REAL MONEY

REAL MONEY

ROBERT LYLE

ANCHOR BOOKS
Anchor Press/Doubleday, Garden City, New York
1976

Anchor Books Edition 1976

Library of Congress Cataloging in Publication Data

Lyle, Robert.
Real money.

Bibliography: p. 177
Includes index.
1. Money—United States. 2. Inflation (Finance)—United States. 3. United States—Economic conditions—1961– I. Title.
HG538.L94 332.4′973
ISBN 0-385-11352-8
Library of Congress Catalog Card Number 75–17070

Printed in the United States of America

To Lexi for her love
Ida for her faith

CONTENTS

ACKNOWLEDGMENTS

I can never fully express my appreciation to the many government officials, bankers, stockbrokers, accountants, attorneys, investment consultants, and investors who spent many hours with me in candid conversation and who gave of their time, resources, wisdom, and good offices in making this book possible.

To these, then, and to those others who could not be named, my special thanks: Alan Abelson, *Barron's;* Jodey T. Allen, Mathematica, Inc.; Robert Aron, J. Aron & Company; Lawrence Baker, California Chief Deputy Insurance Commissioner; Ashby Bladen, Executive Vice President, Guardian Life Insurance Company; Arch Booth, president, Chamber of Commerce of the United States; Peter Brookhouse; Lester Brown, U. S. Department of Agriculture; James Carter, Federal Deposit Insurance Corporation; Louis Chairman, Builders' Association of Greater Boston; Sebastian Dangerfield, Ph.D.; Sam Dunn; Michael Edgar, vice president, Morgan Guaranty Trust; John R. Evans, commissioner, Securities and Exchange Commission; Milton Friedman, Ph.D., University of Chicago; Ray D. Garrett, Jr., chairman, Securities and Exchange Commission; Norman H. Grant, Securities Investor Protection Corporation; Robert Heilbroner; José Ramon Hernández, Embassy of the Republic of Venezuela; Richard H. Jenrette; George Kaufman, Ph.D., University of Oregon; Dr. John Knowles, president, The Rockefeller Foundation; Charles A. McDonald, Office of Wage Stabilization; J. James McKennan, Public Defender, Montgomery County, Maryland; Frank McKnight, Commodity Credit Corporation; J. Mentor; Arthur M. Okun, Brookings Institution; Robert Pipski, district manager, Matthey Bishop; Norman Poser, Securities and Exchange Commission; James W. Price, New York Stock Exchange; Senator William Proxmire; Sidney Rolfe, *Saturday Review;* Dennis Shattuck; D. Garret Shook; Ted Soll, A. A. Sommer, Jr., Securities and Exchange Commission; Leonard Spacek, CPA, Arthur Andersen & Company; David Steinberg; Henry B. Turner, former Assistant U. S. Secretary of Commerce; Lester Wiles, American Petroleum Institute.

Finally, my thanks to Sharon McKern and Lana Pipes for their valuable research and preparation of the manuscript and to David Thomas for his continuing technical assistance.

INTRODUCTION

No matter how you view it, these are unusual economic times. The guideposts and benchmarks along the financial road we all travel from our first dollar on toward retirement have been moved or swept away.

A penny saved, once a penny earned, now becomes less than it was yesterday. Money placed in savings accounts withers away as prices outpace the highest savings interest allowed by law. The stock market, not long ago a way to invest with some chance of success, lies a shambles after stripping away the savings of thousands.

Social Security, the financial port of last resort for millions, balances on the brink of insolvency with only enough reserves *today* to meet its obligations for eight months. Unless extraordinary measures are taken, the Social Security System will be bankrupt before 1980.

At last count our national debt was $490 billion and rising, a worsening economic vital sign that can not be ignored as though it would go away. The interest on our national debt, and eventually the principal, *must* be paid if our economic system is to survive.

Neither Congress nor the President was able to put forth a fiscal 1976 budget which produced less than a

$70-billion deficit. Election year tax cuts proposed by the President in October 1975 would raise the fiscal 1977 budget to $395 billion, compared to the estimated $370 billion for fiscal 1976. It seems that the only emergency measure left to buy time for the failing U.S. economy is to risk bleeding it to death.

The hidden economic signposts established by time and proven experience still remain, even though the makeshift guidelines established by the framers of our managed economy are gone. The power and financial protection of "real money" remains as valid today as it has during every economic crisis since the beginning of modern history.

Some economists and politicians are convinced the fate of America was doomed from the day Presidents and politicians attempted to transform the federal budget from a tool for fiscal management into an instrument of social science in the name of a "New Deal," a "Fair Deal," or, more recently, the "Great Society" of the Johnson administration.

Other respected authorities state that our vote for national self-destruction was cast in 1942 when the United States once again decided to make the world "safe for democracy." Still others, more familiar with today's newspapers than history, simply blame the Near East oil sheiks and let it go at that.

Whatever the cause of our economic plight, the effect upon your lifestyle can be devastating if you continue to leave your economic future in the hands of those who brought the economy you live in to its present state of disarray.

There is a way out. It will mean cutting away from the herd. It will require an understanding of how we were manipulated to where we are. It will mean turning a deaf ear to "authorities," the "experts" and "spokesmen" whose advice will more often be concerned with political and special interests other than yours.

1

What Is Money?

> *Money is a creature of the law, and the creation of money should be maintained as an exclusive monopoly of the National Government. The privilege of creating and issuing money is not only the supreme prerogative of the Government, it is the Government's greatest privilege.*
>
> Abraham Lincoln, 1863

What President Lincoln said, speaking on the occasion of signing into law the National Bank Act of 1863, is an indication of the tragic misunderstanding which most people, including too many government leaders, have about money.

Currency and coins are "creatures of law" and the nations which issue them, but money—*real money*—is outside the province of government and can neither be created nor devalued by legislation nor edict, nor even by force of military or economic dictatorship.

In our acceptance of paper currency as money, we have lost sight of the fact that currency and coins are merely *receipts* for real money (gold and silver), which is supposed to be in storage somewhere.

Theoretically, we are supposed to be able to exchange

currency for real money, but almost from the beginning of modern civilization those who placed their wealth in currency rather than real money lived to regret giving control of their financial resources to others.

During the 1590s, in the days when Shakespeare was busy writing *Midsummer Night's Dream,* it was customary for Europeans to deposit their gold with goldsmiths, who were the best equipped to safeguard it. The goldsmiths gave each depositor a receipt for his gold.

As time went by, these receipts for gold came to be accepted exactly as gold had been. They could be traded for goods and services *as though* they were gold. Horses could be bought, land could be purchased, and taxes could be paid with these receipts. Everyone accepted them because everyone knew that they could exchange them for anything that gold could purchase. Besides, the gold—the real money—was in safekeeping and could always be claimed by merely presenting the receipt to the goldsmith who issued it.

The goldsmiths' receipts for gold soon began circulating as paper money.

It wasn't long before the goldsmiths realized that they were in a position to make money by lending gold they didn't have. Few people came in to claim their gold at the same time, so the goldsmiths wondered why they could not issue receipts for gold to people for a fixed period of time and exact a percentage of the face value as a service charge?

Needless to say, the idea was a popular one (especially with the goldsmiths), and soon there were many more receipts for gold circulating than there was gold in the goldsmiths' safes to back them.

This was the beginning of the "fractional" banking system that exists to this day. (During the fall of 1974, the United States dollar was backed only 5 per cent by gold.)

Under the fractional banking system of the goldsmiths, money was available to meet the needs of the economy, but if business conditions took a turn for the worse and people began turning in their gold receipts for real money all at once, the whole system could collapse.

Even in the limited economy of the 1600s, two major flaws in the goldsmith banking system soon became apparent:

1. There was nothing to keep the goldsmiths from issuing limitless numbers of receipts for gold.

2. A goldsmith's receipts were accepted only in the area where he was known; no one wanted to risk accepting a receipt from a goldsmith who might not exist.

Gradually, as printing methods and papermaking improved and as the idea of currency caught on, governments began issuing paper money. The theory was the same as with goldsmith banking: the currency was merely a "receipt" for gold and silver in the governments' vaults. The real money could be claimed at any time.

Government currency solved problem number two pretty well. A nation's currency was accepted anywhere within its borders. It failed, however, to solve problem number one.

Americans' painful association with paper currency began in the early days of our revolution and it continues to this day.

When the thirteen colonies banded together to seek their independence from the government of King George III, the Continental Congress issued our first "national" currency (some of the colonies had issued their own paper money earlier), called "Continental" dollars.

The colonists took it on faith that the central colonial treasury held sufficient gold and silver on deposit to back its new money, but as the war wore on the Congress printed more and more currency, until the Continental dollar was considered almost without value.

The first Continental currency was issued by the Congress in August of 1775, and by the following spring each Continental was worth fifty cents. Within four years, by the spring of 1779, it had the purchasing power of only three cents.

Colonists who kept their funds in real money fared considerably better than those who maintained blind faith in the Congress's promises of a sound currency. Paper dollars, during that cold winter of 1779, were traded for the limited supply of silver dollars at the rate of five hundred to one.

During the summer of 1779 the Congress issued new currency, exchangeable for the original Continentals at the rate of twenty of the old for one of the new, but the new currency depreciated 50 per cent within six months.

As if to warn those who might put too much faith in the value of the dollar, some of the currency issued by the Continental Congress bore the Latin phrase *Exitus in Dubio Est,* or "The end is in doubt."

The Continental dollar's most remembered contribution to our history is the phrase "not worth a Continental."

Americans populating the land at the time of the Civil War were the next victims whose hard-earned incomes and savings were wiped out by paper currency.

Duplicating to an extent the process of the goldsmith

bankers, many local banks during the 1860s issued their own inadequately backed currency, which brought on bank failures and local recessions. In an effort to stem the problem once and for all, Congress passed the National Bank Act of 1863, which required all banks to obtain charters from the federal government and to operate under government rules and regulations.

The newly chartered and supposedly controlled banks were still allowed to print currency for a time. These inflationary new national bank notes, paper currency with little backing in real money, touched off price increases of nearly 120 per cent in four years and brought on the great depression of 1873—which lasted until 1879.

Again, during the 1860s, those who held the real money of the time—gold and silver coins and bars of the precious metals—managed to hold their own against the effect of inflationary currency upon their purchasing power and savings. The price of gold rose 185 per cent against living cost increases of "only" 120 per cent. The increased price of silver, though not so great as that of gold, insulated its owners relatively well from the paper currency wolf which consumed the resources of many.

Congress sought to cure the depression of 1873 with yet another dose of paper currency, but had its hand stayed from turning on the presses by the veto of President Ulysses S. Grant.

In 1879 the country returned to a precious-metal standard for its currency. Inflation had been turned back and price levels remained stable for one of the longest periods in American history. But price stability was due as much to resources coming into the country as it was to any supposedly sound federal monetary policy.

The late 1800s and early 1900s were times of mass immigration from Europe and the United States gained the productivity of many German artisans and industrial workers, skilled Scandinavian farmers drawn by new homestead legislation, plus the cheap labor of newly arrived Italians and eastern Europeans who fled to the United States to escape grinding poverty at home. These immigrants, which first gave rise to some people calling our country "the melting pot of nations," increased the contemporary American labor force by nearly one third at far less than the cost of training or paying native-born workers.

The Spanish-American War of 1898 freed Cuba and Puerto Rico from Spain and brought the latter to the United States. Cuba soon gained its independence, but only under treaty provisions with the United States that made the island easy prey for exploitation.

By ignoring the social costs of its economic expansion, America became convinced that it had at long last achieved continuing prosperity and a "sound dollar." We were to make nearly the same mistake again during the 1960s and early 1970s by ignoring the effects of "exporting" United States inflation to Europe.

When Congress established the Federal Reserve System in 1913, after behind-the-scenes groundwork by bankers, which economist H. S. Kenan (in *The Federal Reserve Bank,* Noontide Press, 1968) called "fraudulent, unconstitutional, and surreptitious," the government withdrew the national banks' right to issue banknote currency. In addition, the Federal Reserve Act took away by congressional consent Congress's direct control over the monetary system. Article I, Section 8, Paragraph 5 of the Constitution states that Congress shall have the power "to coin money, regulate the value thereof and of foreign coin . . ."

What the Federal Reserve Act did was to place control over the issue of Unites States money in the hands of *private bankers* who are neither elected by nor answerable to the Congress or the people of the United States.

The system of checks and balances so valued by the founders of our nation had been circumvented by men who stood to profit enormously by the maneuver—at your expense.

When the Federal Reserve system was organized in 1913, the total supply of money in the United States was $12 billion. By 1929, the beginning of the most recent great depression, the money supply had grown to $26 billion. By 1973 the total money supply had been inflated to $571 billion. The increased supply of money didn't come from anywhere: it was simply *printed.*

In 1929 our currency was backed 11 per cent by gold; nine dollars of paper currency were in circulation for every dollar of gold in the vaults of the U. S. Treasury. By 1972 each paper dollar was backed only 5 per cent by gold. As of December 31, 1972, there were 943 paper dollars in circulation for every ounce of gold in government vaults, then valued at $38 per ounce. Almost no one needs to be told that the dollar is worth less now than it was during the worst of the so-called Great Depression of 1929–39.

But we Americans aren't the only ones in recent history to feel ourselves standing helplessly in the wings while events beyond our reach cause our purchasing power and savings to dwindle before our eyes.

Even more disastrous was what happened to the people of Germany when their government set its printing presses at high speed in the aftermath of World War I. Before the "war to end all wars," the exchange rate was four marks for one dollar. The value of the mark dropped from 4.2 per dollar to 76.7 between July 1914 and July 1921. Then the bottom dropped out:

	MARKS PER $
January 1922	191.8
July 1922	493.2
January 1923	17,972.0
July 1923	353,412.0
August 1923	4,620,455.0
September 1923	98,860,000.0
October 1923	25,260,208,000.0
November 15, 1923	4,200,000,000,000.0

Other European currencies were sucked into the whirlpool along with the sinking German mark. Austrian, Hungarian, and Polish currencies became worth less than the paper they were printed on. They were eventually rehabilitated by their governments at rates of from $1/_{14,000}$ to $1/_{1,800,000}$ to 1.

For some Germans at least, the ownership of gold and silver coins often meant the difference between life and death. A single gold mark came to be worth more than one trillion paper ones, and scarcity made its purchasing power far greater even than that.

More recently, the citizens of many countries have been given cause to question the wisdom of holding their savings in paper currency.

Brazil devalued its currency five times during 1974—thirty-three times since 1968. The British pound sterling was devalued from $4.00 to $2.80 in 1949 and again to

$2.40 in 1967. The French franc was devalued by 11 per cent in 1969.

The United States dollar was devalued 40 per cent against gold by President Franklin D. Roosevelt on January 30, 1934, the price of gold rising from $20.67 an ounce to $35.00. When Roosevelt asked Senator Carter Glass what he thought of the move, Glass replied, "I think it is worse than anything Ali Baba's forty thieves ever perpetrated."

The dollar/gold exchange rate remained at $35.00 for thirty-seven years. President Richard Nixon devalued the dollar twice. On December 18, 1971, the dollar was devalued 7.89 per cent against gold, which was pegged at $38.00 an ounce. On February 12, 1972, President Nixon's decision to devalue the dollar further was announced by Treasury Secretary George P. Shultz. Gold's new official value against the dollar rose to $42.22 an ounce.

Of course, this didn't mean Americans could exchange $42.22 in paper currency for an ounce of gold. The United States Government had outlawed ownership of gold by its citizens in 1933. Since August 15, 1971, the government had declined even to honor the claims of foreign central banks which presented paper dollars to be exchanged for gold. The new $42.22 rate was merely the latest figure at which the United States *refused* to exchange gold for currency.

Today America ranks among the lower half of nations with respect to the strength (gold backing) of its currency. U.S. currency has less than half the gold backing of the German mark—5 per cent gold backing for the dollar compared with 10.15 per cent for the mark.

Here are a few other currencies which, according to the computations of economist Harry Browne, outstrip the dollar in gold backing:

	% BACKING 1975
Lebanese pound	40.80
Swiss franc	22.11
Portuguese escudo	17.91
Austrian schilling	17.55
Dutch guilder	17.20
South African rand	15.35
Belgian franc	12.77
West German deutschmark	10.15
French franc	6.29
Swedish krona	4.84

If money is to be something you can count upon—a medium of exchange you will be able to "trade" in the future for something of value—then clearly the currency in your pocket or purse or in your savings account is not real money because devaluation by the government can make it practically worthless.

Through continued printing of paper currency without increasing its reserves of monetary gold and silver, a government can extend its inflationary hand into the vault of the strongest bank, can invade the most secure safety deposit box, and can lift your wallet or purse with greater stealth than the smoothest pickpocket.

Without warning, any President of the United States can devalue the world-wide acceptance of your currency, making nearly everything cost more.

If the currency most of us are used to thinking of as money isn't money at all, then what *is* money?

For thousands of years gold and silver have been the universally accepted medium of exchange. No Congress nor President, no King nor Parliament can debase their value nor destroy the acceptance of gold and silver as real money.

In a time of impending monetary crisis, perhaps the truest advice of all can still be found on the face of the Continental Congress one-sixth dollar note printed nearly two hundred years ago: "Mind Your Business."

2

The Day the Economy Stopped Running

> *A return to either price stability or financial stability without an intervening crash appears to me to be practically impossible. And the longer the crash is postponed by continuing the inflationary process—the worse it will be when it does come.*
>
> Ashby Bladen, Executive Vice President, Guardian Life Insurance Company, 1974

There was a time not many months ago when concern about a coming crash would be written off by many people as just another "doomsday" pronouncement almost on a par with marching barefoot in the streets wearing a long robe and carrying a sign saying REPENT, THE END IS NEAR.

Today increasing numbers of economists are beginning to feel that the end *is* near—and that it's already too late to repent.

On July 15, 1974, the Washington *Post* reported: "No one with sound credentials has talked seriously about financial collapse and depression for decades. Now knowledgeable people are quoting odds."

"The more I think about it," says Arthur M. Okun of

the Brookings Institution, "the more vivid it becomes. It's not a scenario you can laugh at anymore."

Alan Greenspan, shortly before he became head of President Gerald R. Ford's Council of Economic Advisers, said that he sees

> very major potential dangers; we are so far outside the realm of historical experience that I don't know how to assess the probabilities.
>
> Take all this talk of a depression and social breakdown and all the other horror stories. I can't present any solid reasons why these frightening scenarios cannot happen, which means they possibly could happen. This is the first time I've felt that way since the start of my professional career.

Dr. Arthur F. Burns, chairman of the Board of Governors of the Federal Reserve System, has warned that "if long continued, inflation at anything like its present rate would threaten the very foundations of our society." (When Dr. Burns spoke, during the summer of 1973, the national inflation rate was 8.8 per cent.)

Whether Dr. Burns was addressing himself to that fact or not, money has historically functioned as the foundation of society as we define it. The brotherhood of man has faltered, as time and time again tribe turned against tribe and nation against nation. But money, in whatever medium of exchange, has endured.

The form hasn't always been the same. Primitive man at one time or another used arrow poison, boar's tusks, throwing disks, grain, ostrich feathers, pig's jawbones, salt, spearheads, tar, whale's teeth, and even woodpecker scalps as media of exchange.

Perhaps the most improbable "coins of the realm" were the multiton, twelve-foot-in-diameter circular stones used by some Oceanic cultures. Immovable as well as indestructable, they never changed hands but merely "belonged" to the owner of record even though he never took possession.

During the colonial years of this country, beaver and buffalo skins and tobacco served as legal tender. Throughout history only gold and silver have endured as universally accepted means of exchange.

Today, though U.S. paper currency has no intrinsic value and will not be redeemed by the U. S. Treasury for *anything*—except, perhaps, a tax receipt—we think of it as money.

Rhoda Koenig, in the November 1973 issue of *Harper's,* wrote:

> I like my money nice and live. Every two weeks I cash my paycheck and walk the two blocks to my bank with a bulging wallet, feeling sexy, accomplished, and invulnerable. Sometimes I take it in $100 bills, and one happy day I walked the distance with a single $500 bill. I felt like a combination of Mae West, Consuelo Vanderbilt, and Calamity Jane. I wanted to tuck the $500 bill in my waistband. I wanted to seduce a traffic cop. I wanted to go into a drugstore and buy a package of gum.

In our gut we feel there is nothing money cannot do. It can take us anywhere and buy us anything—or anybody. It purchases a thousand options. It makes us stronger in influence if not in physical strength. Enough of it buys freedom and joy and better health.

Money has yet to buy its last ambassadorship or sway its last congressional vote or bring down its last national government. All these and more each of us could buy with money, if we but had enough.

With money we can substitute pleasure for pain, we can stay the flow of tears, banish unhappiness beyond the far horizon, and flee from winter's grasp into the soft and fragrant embrace of spring.

The mere possession of riches smooths the way of the wealthy without their even having to spend any of it. The wealthy are sought out, catered to, and welcomed everywhere.

There is something magical about money which affects us all. When we contemplate great wealth, we feel it in the same place we feel a sexual turn-on.

Yet for all the magical properties we give it, money is in trouble—and, as Dr. Burns said, the decline of "money" threatens the foundations of our society.

We have put our trust in paper currency which is backed only 5 per cent by gold. We have put our trust in paper currency which can be devalued without warning. We have put our trust in paper currency which is losing its value faster than any institution can shore it up. We have put our trust in paper currency—and we have called it "money."

The federal government in 1933 declared that its citizens could no longer redeem dollars for gold. In 1968 it told us that "silver certificates" would no longer be redeemed for silver.

On August 15, 1971, President Nixon announced to the world that the United States Government would no longer exchange gold for the billions of paper dollars held by foreign central banks. The President, in effect, issued a surprise "stop payment" on U.S. currency in the hands of foreign governments.

Between 1964 and 1968 the Johnson administration increased the supply of "printing-press" money 47 per cent. Between 1969 and 1973 the supply of money increased 49 per cent.

During that time there was not one ounce of gold or silver added to the national treasury. The federal government simply printed more dollars while the national debt grew to about $458 billion.

What is happening? The price of everything *isn't* going up. The value of the dollar is going *down.* In many respects, the effect on family budgets is the same, but it's important to recognize the difference because the difference offers a way out. The difference offers a way for informed people to protect themselves from inflation during times of monetary crisis.

Nineteen Seventy-Four's "galloping" inflation, so defined that year by Federal Reserve chairman Arthur Burns, costs us more than vanishing savings and a lowered standard of living. It robs us of our power to control our own lives and leaves us feeling helpless to save ourselves from whatever economic monster is loose in the streets.

College education for many is shading from "assured" to "doubtful" and darkening to "impossible" under the onslaught of inflation. Homes and businesses planned and saved for drift agonizingly beyond the financial grasp of many. Vacations and other pleasures of life on which Americans spend discretionary income must be delayed, perhaps forever, as discretionary income is whittled down to nothing by the increasing cost of essentials.

By October of 1974, 67 per cent of American families reported that inflation had imposed changes in their lifestyles. Among individuals, almost 55 per cent were worried about inflation wiping out their savings.

Forty-five per cent said they expected a depression at least as bad as that of the 1930s.

By 1974 the dollar depreciated to less than half its 1949 value. A 1974 yearly income of $21,000 was required to match the purchasing power of $10,000 in 1949.

Prices in the United States "rose" nearly 11 per cent during the *first half* of 1974. The cost of purchasing even the bare essentials had become so great that a family of four found themselves with almost no discretionary income.

The March 17, 1975, issue of *U.S. News & World Report* predicted that within twenty-five years the average American family could expect to spend $622,000 for a new home, $45,000 for a year of college, $167 for a pair of man's shoes, $8.00 for a movie and more than $20.00 for a man's haircut. Just to make ends meet at the level of a $14,000 income during 1974, a family during the year 2000 will need to earn a minimum of $112,000.

Serious crime in the United States rose 16 per cent during the first half of 1974 and law enforcement officials attributed most of the rise to inflation.

"I think people in general are getting really desperate," feels Montgomery County, Maryland, chief public defender J. James McKennan, whose county experienced a 24.7 increase in crime over the first half of 1973.

Robert Conger, director of the FBI's crime reporting section says, "A lot of big-city police chiefs are saying that unemployment and inflation are big factors. Unemployment is up 30 to 35 per cent among young blacks and whites in some of the major cities."

According to the October 4, 1974, Washington *Post*,

Godfrey Fergeson of that city admitted stealing four loaves of Wonder Bread for his sister. "Bread," Fergeson told the arresting officers, "is so expensive."

For those who still have money for food, the menu from which to choose is becoming increasingly short—and expensive. Steak has been replaced by hamburger and hamburger is being replaced by "TVP," texturized vegetable protein. We are gradually losing the freedom to travel as the price of autos, tires, and gasoline rises, to prohibit all but the most essential driving.

Housing costs have priced the single-family dwelling out of the reach of families who just a few years ago were saving for a house in the suburbs. Today their savings are gone and the house is too expensive.

Inflation is making the decisions, narrowing the choices, and cutting the options. As it continues, many of our freedoms—to work at employment we choose, to live where we choose, and to do as we choose with our property and our earnings—will disappear.

Inflation—8.8 per cent when the following study was made during mid-1973—was eating away at conventional investments so fast their earning rates were unable to keep up:

$10,000 invested during mid-1973 in six-month 5.3 per cent U. S. Treasury bills was worth only $9,840 one year later.

$10,000 invested during mid-1973 in 5 per cent tax-exempt municipal bonds was worth only $9,630 by mid-1974.

$10,000 invested during mid-1973 in ordinary 5.5 per cent passbook savings (assuming a 50 per cent tax on interest) yielded only $9,470.

$10,000 invested during mid-1973 in one-year

certificates of deposit at 5.8 per cent yielded only $9,460 after taxes.

$10,000 invested during mid-1973 in 8 per cent corporate bonds net only $9,330 in mid-1974 after taxes.

$10,000 invested during mid-1973 in 5.7 per cent long-term Treasury bonds left you with only $8,770 in purchasing power 12 months later.

$10,000 invested in representative stocks from Standard & Poor's industrials during mid-1973 were worth only $8,040 by mid-1974.

$10,000 invested during mid-1973 in Standard & Poor's utilities would have shrunk to a mere $7,750 by mid-1974.

The flight of money from the stock market during 1974 dragged the "blue-chip" Dow-Jones average down to a low of 584.56 on October 4.

The September 9, 1974, issue of *U.S. News & World Report* reported that losses by the nation's 31 million stockholders had topped $500 billion since January 1973. "Bond values," reported *U.S. News,* dropped billions at the same time."

Officials of the Federal Savings and Loan Insurance Corporation (FSLIC) reported that during 1974 "billions of dollars took flight from the nation's savings banks and savings and loan associations in the face of inflation rates which exceed interest which could have been paid on savings accounts."

In actions that looked like opening blows in the first round of a heavyweight bout, the U. S. Treasury and two of New York's largest banks fought it out during the summer of 1974 for America's investment and savings dollars.

On July 24 Citicorp, which controls Citibank, New York's largest bank, offered—and quickly sold out—

$650 million in variable-interest notes pegged 1.25 percentile points above the average rate on three-month Treasury bills.

Less than two weeks later, the Chase Manhattan Bank was swamped with buyers for its own $200-million issue of variable interest notes similar to Citibank's.

Then, on August 6, the U. S. Treasury offered—and quickly sold out—$4 billion in Treasury notes paying up to 9 per cent interest.

Soon bank holding companies in nearly every major city were girding to do battle with the Treasury's 9 per cent notes. Continental Illinois announced plans to issue a $125 million note offering; Alabama Bancorp said it would offer $25 million; First Security Company of Salt Lake City revealed plans to sell $20 million. California's Crocker National Bank, the Philadelphia National Bank, and First Piedmont, climbed through the ropes and into the ring to join the free-for-all.

With interest rates chasing each other up a spiral staircase, savings banks—prevented by government regulation from offering competing interest—turned to Capitol Hill and yelled "Foul!"

Before the month was over, both Senate and House banking committees passed legislation allowing the Federal Reserve Board to set maximum rates which banks could pay on variable-interest notes.

But much of the damage, as appraised by savings and loan bankers, had been done. More than $1,215 billion had been effectively removed from reserves S & L's could count on to finance home mortgages. By September 1974, housing starts sank to their lowest point in five years.

Money, the common denominator by which society exchanged value for value, was losing its value faster than almost any available means could be devised for protecting it. In the face of late 1974's 12 per cent inflation rate, 9 per cent Treasury bills and variable-interest bank notes pegged to similar rates of interest became merely ways of losing less than in other investments.

Only investors in precious metals and a few foreign currencies have been able to weather the worsening economic hurricane without financial loss. The Swiss franc appreciated 42 per cent against the dollar from 1970 through 1974. Ten thousand dollars invested in silver bullion during mid-1973 would have netted its owner more than $15,000 by mid-1974.

Paper dollars, the medium of exchange most Americans still think of as money, continue to lose ground as U.S. federal economic planners budget increased annual deficits. A minimum $70-billion deficit was built into federal budget for fiscal 1976 (which runs from July 1, 1975, through June 30, 1976), and even larger deficits for fiscal 1977 were being proposed by the President during the fall of 1975.

The $70-billion fiscal 1976 budget compares depressingly with the fiscal 1967 budget of the first of the Johnson administration's "guns and butter" years of Vietnam military expenditures and "Great Society" social programs.

Reduced tax revenues resulting from the 1973–75 recession, Congress's $28-billion tax cut, unemployment payments, and federally funded emergency employment programs cast the mold for continuing inflation into the late 1970s, the 1980s, and perhaps beyond.

National unemployment, seldom the running mate of inflation, reached 8.7 per cent by April 1975.

Our government is cornered into meeting the demands of a population which wants "no inflation" and "no unemployment" at the same time. The time has passed when either can be delivered without paying the unacceptable cost of continuing inflation.

Congress in 1975 is attempting to "bail out" various segments of the economy—housing, savings banks, the unemployed, and others by resorting to deficit-spending programs which could touch off the greatest dollar inflation in the memory of anyone now living.

"There is precious little support for unemployment," a member of the U. S. Senate told me recently. "There isn't a politician in Washington who will risk being associated with legislation which will result in significant unemployment. More inflation is the only road they'll take."

A national survey taken shortly before the November 1974 election indicated that 53 per cent of the American people favored wage and price controls as a means of halting inflation. During the first half of 1975 members of both the House and Senate still argued for wage and price controls to halt the cost of living.

But the record shows that in the month following the end of the Nixon administration's ninety-day wage-and-price control experiment, the cost of living shot up at a 22.8 per cent annual rate. Looking back, almost every responsible economist feels that wage and price controls only act to create crippling shortages and add fuel to the inflationary fire.

According to President Nixon (as late as April 1974), America had no cause to fear an inflationary firestorm. "The economy," he told the nation, "will begin to move forward again" during the last six months of 1974. He assured all Americans that, over all, 1974 would be a "good year" economically, that 1975 would be a "very good year," and that 1976 would be "the best year in America's history, the most prosperous, the most free."

In October of 1974 Secretary of Commerce Frederick B. Dent reassured America that there was nothing to worry about. The economic downturn which started in late 1973, he explained, was nothing more than a "sideways waffle" passing through the economy.

The following month the Commerce Department announced that the September index of economic indicators had nose-dived more sharply than at any time since 1951. President Ford admitted, "We are facing some difficult circumstances." But a month later he was still maintaining that "our country is not in an economic crisis."

On January 15, 1975, in his State of the Union message to the Congress, President Ford's news was more somber: "I must say to you that the State of the Union is not good. Millions of Americans are out of work. Recession and inflation are eroding the money of millions more. Prices are too high and sales are too slow."

By March of 1975 Treasury Secretary William E. Simon made a prediction: "I think we'll see the bottom in the middle months of this year, with the upturn continuing and strengthening into 1976."

The appraisal of British economist and author Harry Schultze is more realistic: "Paper money and its buying power will continue to fall like the bones of prehistoric animals into the La Brea tar pits."

3

The Case Against the Federal Reserve

The Board of Governors of the Federal Reserve System opposes any bill which proposes a stable price level.
Marriner S. Eccles, Chairman, Board of
Governors of the Federal Reserve System, 1936–48

On the evening of November 22, 1910, a passenger train bearing the private railroad car of Senator Nelson Aldrich pulled out of the Hoboken, New Jersey, railroad station. During the next day and a half, it was to carry the car and its occupants away from the grim Northeast, already touched by winter, to the more warmly hospitable and still-green countryside of Georgia.

Aboard the car with Senator Aldrich were: Assistant Secretary of the Treasury A. Piatt Andrew, Jr.; Henry P. Davison, senior partner of J. P. Morgan & Company; Charles D. Norton, president of the First National Bank of New York; Frank H. Vanderlip, president of the National City Bank of New York; and Paul M. Warburg, an immigrant and former member of the powerful German banking house of M. M. Warburg & Company and now a $500,000-a-year partner in the influential New York banking house of Kuhn, Loeb & Company.

Their meeting, held in secret at the Jekyll Island (Georgia) Hunt Club, was for the purpose of developing plans to:

1. Usurp from Congress its constitutional right to issue money;

2. Take control of the money supply in the United States;

3. Assure that vast millions of dollars in annual interest on the national debt would be paid to private bankers.

Their scheme was a successful conspiracy which makes the recent Watergate scandal look like a foul-up caper attempted by "the gang that couldn't shoot straight."

Senator Aldrich came to his private car that November night fresh from a year in Europe as head of the National Monetary Commission, created by Congress in the aftermath of the bank panic of 1907. Since returning to the United States, the senator had made no report to Congress, had released no statement to the press, and steadfastly refused to talk about the findings of the Commission's two-year study of European banking systems.

The secret meeting at J. P. Morgan's exclusive Jekyll Island Hunt Club was to make available and place into motion for private bankers' advantage all that Aldrich had learned on his European tour.

Why the secrecy? Because any monetary reform passed by Congress which was not written by and for the private bankers would be the beginning of the end of their powerful personal fortunes.

Senator Aldrich and the chosen band of private

bankers had gone to Jekyll Island to write legislation which would be passed by Congress and signed into law by President Woodrow Wilson as the Federal Reserve Act of 1913.

Three of the necessary requirements for any new central bank, stated Warburg, were:

1. That it be owned by private individuals who would profit from ownership of shares;

2. That it would control the nation's total financial resources;

3. That it would control the issue of money.

Warburg also warned that the term "central bank" was to be avoided at all costs, since it would remind the public of the great privately owned central banks of Europe. Warburg proposed the term "Federal Reserve Bank." He suggested too that there be several regional Federal Reserve Banks to further disassociate the new system from European central banks so disliked by the public.

Inclusion of the proposed regional banks in the legislation actually meant very little, since the vast amount of money and power concentrated in the Northeast made the branches impotent dependents upon the New York Federal Reserve Bank.

Senator Aldrich, familiar with the threat of possible congressional investigation, proposed that all officials of the Federal Reserve Bank should be *appointive* offices.

The bankers' plan to gain control of the American money supply did not move forward entirely without opposition. *Harper's Weekly,* dated May 7, 1910, stated:

> Finance and tariff are reserved by Nelson Aldrich as falling within his sole purview and jurisdiction.

> Mr. Aldrich is endeavoring to devise, through the National Monetary Commission, a banking and currency law. A great many hundred thousands of Americans are firmly convinced that Mr. Aldrich sums up in his personality the greatest and most sinister menace to the welfare of the United States.

Wilbur Stones, writing in the September 10, 1911, edition of the *North American Review*, said:

> Senator Aldrich would take from the people and give to the bankers absolute control of the peoples' money. It is apparent that in such a body of bankers there would be no opportunity for the people or their representatives to make their wishes known effectively, if those wishes conflicted with those of the banking interests.

Minnesota Congressman Charles A. Lindbergh stated on the floor of the House of Representatives on December 5, 1911, that:

> The Aldrich Plan is the Wall Street Plan. It is a broad challenge to the government by the money trust. . . . It was by a very clever move [after the bank-caused panic of 1907] that the National Monetary Commission was created. . . . The real purpose was to get a Monetary Commission which would frame a proposition for amendments to our currency and banking laws which would suit the money trust. . . .

In response to a reporter's question about an anti-Aldrich Plan speech by Senator Robert M. La Follette of Wisconsin in which the senator stated that "a money trust of not more than fifty men controls the nation," a parner of banker J. P. Morgan replied that the senator was in error.

"I personally know," said Morgan partner G. F. Baker, "that no more than eight men run this country."

The spotlight focused on the Aldrich plan by editorial outcry and the speeches of opposition legislators led to a congressional investigation of the plan by a committee headed by Louisiana Representative Arsène Pujo. But pressure upon the committee by financial interests struck its members dumb and blind, and they did not ask a dozen questions during months of investigation. Their time was consumed listening to pro-Aldrich witnesses lined up by the bankers and their allies in Congress.

The framers of the Federal Reserve Act did not put together their banking bill mindless of a "captive" ally in the White House.

President Woodrow Wilson had first come to the attention of the New York bankers while serving as president of Princeton University. During the bank panic of 1907, Wilson had declared that "all of this trouble could have been averted if we appointed a committee of six or seven public-spirited men like J. P. Morgan to handle the affairs of our country."

Soon Wilson was being invited into the drawing rooms of the rich and powerful, who later bought him the governorship of New Jersey and, in 1912, the presidency of the United States. Wilson signed the Federal Reserve Act into law on December 23, 1913.

We will return to the subject again, but it is worth noting here that during 1974, the national debt surpassed $490 billion. Annual interest on the national debt, paid mostly to stockholders of the Federal Reserve System, now exceeds $27 billion.

An understanding of how the Federal Reserve System operates is important because, like it or not, the

"Fed"—as bankers call it—is the axis around which revolves the monetary system of the United States. As such, it is in a position to greatly affect the value of your income and savings.

The legacy which the Aldrich plan left us provides for twelve regional branches of the Federal Reserve Bank. Each of the regional Federal Reserve Banks is governed by nine directors, *six* of whom are selected directly from among the directors of *privately owned* banks in each region.

The president of each regional Federal Reserve Bank is elected by the board of each regional bank, the majority of whom are *private bankers*.

Six of the presidents of the twelve regional banks, plus the seven members of the Federal Reserve Board, comprise the membership of the Federal Open Market Committee, a little-known but powerful group of men who meet in Washington every three weeks to determine for the following three weeks and beyond the nation's supply of money and credit and to decide what interest rates are to be.

The origin of the six regional bank presidents we know about: they are elected by the private banker-controlled boards of each regional Fed. The seven members of the Federal Reserve Board who make up the remainder of the Open Market Committee are presidential appointees (ratified by the Senate), who serve fourteen-year terms.

There are several ways in which the members of the Federal Reserve Board and the Federal Open Market Committee can "create" money and thus devalue your currency:

1. They can reduce the ratio of reserves a bank must maintain against loans. Instead of requiring a bank to

have, say, one dollar in its reserve account with the Fed for each ten dollars it is allowed to lend, the Fed can change the ratio to allow the bank to lend *twenty* dollars for each dollar in its reserve account. Thus ten additional dollars have been created out of thin air. (This method is an across-the-board action and, when taken, applies to *all* banks in the system, thus multiplying its inflationary effect.)

2. The Federal Reserve can make a loan to a bank by deciding to increase the amount of the bank's reserve account with the Fed—just the way your bank makes a loan to you by increasing the amount in your checking account. Unlike the deposit your bank adds to your account, the Fed's loan to a bank is "supermoney." Each dollar lent by the Fed to a bank generates additional currency—depending upon the loan-deposit ratio requirement in effect at the time.

The Fed can encourage or discourage borrowing by banks through raising or lowering the "discount rate," the amount of interest which it charges banks for funds which they borrow.

"Changes in bank reserves," according to the Board of Governors of the Federal Reserve System,

> . . . result in a multiple expansion or contraction of bank loans and investments and of the money supply. . . . The lending and investment activities of banks in turn influence conditions in the nation's credit market. Thus actions by the Federal Reserve System to create or extinguish bank reserves not only exert a powerful influence on the flow of bank credit and money, but also have an influence on levels of interest rates and on liquidity and availability of credit in general."

3. The Federal Reserve can also follow a "tight money" policy, making few loans to banks thus driving up the *prime interest rate,* the rate of interest which big banks charge their large corporate borrowers. Interest rates on loans to smaller companies and to individuals are appreciably higher than the "prime" rate.

On a grander scale, the government can create vastly larger amounts of currency out of thin air without changing the loan-deposit ratio or making a loan to any bank.

When the government—often advised by the Federal Reserve bankers—decides that it needs more money, for example, $1 billion:

1. The Secretary of the Treasury tells the Bureau of Engraving and Printing to print $1 billion in government *bonds.*

2. The Federal Reserve Bank tells the Bureau of Engraving and Printing to print $1 billion in Federal Reserve *notes.*

3. The Federal Reserve Bank then *trades* the $1 billion in bonds for $1 billion in Federal Reserve notes.

In actual practice the bonds are funneled through a closely knit group of twenty-one government-authorized bond dealers in a complex process which, in effect, results in the situation we've described above.

Interest on the government bonds is paid by the government to the stockholders of the Federal Reserve Banks. The stockholders of the Federal Reserve Banks are *private banks.* The stockholders of the private banks are *private bankers.*

Marriner S. Eccles, a former chairman of the Board of Governors of the Federal Reserve System, in a letter written to Representative Wright Patman in 1941, stated:

> This so-called stock ownership, however, is more in the nature of an enforced subscription to the capital of the Federal Reserve banks than an ownership in the usual sense. The stock cannot be sold, transferred or hypothecated, nor can it be voted in accordance with the par value of the shares held. Thus the smallest member bank has an equal vote with the largest.
>
> Member banks have no right to participate in earnings above the statuatory dividend. . . .

Money and Banking, by Weldon Welfling, the textbook of the American Institute of Banking, is more candid: "The member banks own the twelve Federal Reserve banks."

If the government can, as we described above, issue bonds, why can't it simply issue currency instead? According to a great many constitutional lawyers and respected economists, it can. One reason why it doesn't was stated by Thomas A. Edison some time ago. "If our nation can issue a dollar bond," said Edison,

> it can issue a dollar bill. The element that makes the bond good makes the bill good also. . . . It is absurd to say that our country can issue $30 million in bonds and not $30 million in currency. Both are promises to pay, but one promise fattens the userers and the other helps the people.

According to Bartow Foundation economist Sebastian Dangerfield, "The owners of banks in the Federal Reserve System are making money out of federal interest payments on the national debt, so it is in their interest to (1) increase the national debt and (2) inflate the amount of currency in circulation, which results in a continuing decrease in the purchasing power of each dollar issued by the Federal Reserve."

As we pointed out earlier, during 1974 the dollar was backed only 5 per cent by gold. In 1928 the dollar's gold backing was 11 per cent. During the five years from 1969 through 1973, the money supply was increased 49 per cent, from $382 to $571 billion, more than double the 22 per cent gain in output of goods. During the decade 1964–73, the money supply was increased 120 per cent.

There is also increasing speculation that, in addition to being an instrument of New York banking interests, the Federal Reserve may be unduly influenced by political expediency. The July 1974 issue of *Fortune* said:

> One of the controversies swirling around the battered Nixon administration has been of special interest to the economics profession. The issue, in brief, is whether the Federal Reserve Board went on a "monetary binge" in 1972 in order to guarantee President Nixon's re-election.
>
> There is at least no doubt about the binge, and there is not much doubt about its consequences either. The Fed created too much money in 1972, and the excess helped to set off the superheated boom of late 1972 and early 1973, which in turn contributed to the outsize inflation rates of 1973 and early 1974.
>
> . . . while the Fed's role seems more decisive all the time, its competence in managing the money supply seems more questionable all the time.

In an interview in the March 1, 1975, issue of *Forbes* magazine, economist Karl Brunner criticized the Federal Reserve for the large gyrations of its monetary policy: "They had this very large 6% acceleration of monetary growth in the first half of last year and practically zero growth in the second half. They accelerated again up to 5% or 6% during October and November, only to slow down in December."

Brunner's own recommendation was for a steady 6 per cent growth rate for the year, but he conceded that the need to finance a record budget deficit would make it difficult for the Federal Reserve to stand firm.

"If we have a total deficit of around $90 billion this year and next, let's suppose the Fed finances a third of that—$30 billion, or $15 billion a year," he said. "That would mean an acceleration in the money growth rate from the current 4% to about 15%. The rate of inflation would go up toward 20% by the end of next year!"

4

The FDIC: Don't Bank on It

At the close of 1974, insured deposits amounted to $520,309 million. The deposit insurance fund totalled $6,124 million, a reserve ratio of 1.18 per cent.

Federal Deposit Insurance Corporation,
Annual Report, 1974

Somewhere in a lower corner of the front window of almost any bank or under the glass top of the stand-up desk where you make out deposit slips and endorse checks is a small sign which says MEMBER FDIC.

Nearly everyone knows that "FDIC" stands for "Federal Deposit Insurance Corporation." We "know" that if the bank where we have our money fails, we will be protected by the FDIC against losses up to the amount of coverage provided on each account.

If you have both a checking and savings account under the same name with a bank, both accounts are considered as one by the FDIC when it comes to figuring the total amount of coverage. If you are a participant in another account at the same bank—say, a joint account—then that account is considered separate and you would also receive the maximum coverage for the current amount of that account. By having several accounts, either with different banks or including different participants, you can considerably increase your right to FDIC account protection.

When the FDIC was created as one of the provisions of the Banking Act of 1935, maximum protection for each insured account was $10,000. The maximum had been increased to $20,000 over the years and on November 27, 1974, maximum protection for each account was raised to $40,000.

In terms of actual purchasing power, however, the new $40,000 limit provided far *less* protection than did the original $10,000.

The FDIC was established in response to public panic in the Great Depression which resulted in the failure of 11,600 banks, more than half the nation's total, during the five years between 1929 and 1933.

The FDIC was sold to the public to quiet its fears and prevent any repetition of a run on banks similar to the one which precipitated the bank failures of the 1930s. The fact is, however, that the FDIC does not maintain a deposit insurance fund which could even begin to protect the public against massive losses in the event of a monetary crisis.

At the close of 1974 the FDIC's total deposit insurance fund amounted to $6,124 million against insured deposits of $520,309 million—an insurance reserve of just over 1 per cent. This is a ratio of around $1.35 for each $100 of insured deposits. In 1934 the FDIC's reserve was $1.84 for every $100 insured.

The 1974 increase in coverage from $20,000 to $40,000 per insured account effectively reduced the FDIC's insurance reserve, since larger claims would be made against the fund should there be another run on the banks.

In the event of a monetary crisis, individuals having claims as the result of widespread bank failures would have to be paid with newly printed inflationary currency.

The FDIC has authority to borrow up to $3 billion from the U. S. Treasury in times of crisis, but that would do little more than perhaps raise its reserve fund to about 2 per cent.

Today, almost all banks in the United States are FDIC-insured. Of the 14,676 commercial and mutual savings banks in existence during 1973, 13,976 were members of the FDIC. There were only 218 uninsured commercial banks in the nation in that year.

The FDIC received its original funding through the purchase of $150 million in FDIC stock by the Treasury. The Federal Reserve bought $139 million. The stock was bought back by the FDIC during 1947 and 1948.

During 1937 the FDIC received almost half its $561 million income from assessments on insured banks and the other half from interest earned on government securities. Bank assessments officially are 1/12 of 1 per cent of each insured bank's deposits. A provision of the Federal Deposit Insurance Act of 1950 provides for adjustments which, during 1973, made each bank's assessment closer to 1/26 of total deposits.

It's interesting to note in passing that the bank and stock market crash which triggered the Great Depression in September 1929 was brought on through the combined inflationary actions of Wall Street brokers and New York bankers.

During the late 1920s major banks of the nation

turned themselves into high-speed money-making machines, through their easy loans to brokers and individuals with get-rich-quick schemes to buy control of America. The process was simplicity itself and, for a time, it worked.

Banks created money by making loans to brokers and individuals which were based upon collateral in the form of stocks purchased with the proceeds of the loans. This easy money made it possible for people to borrow more money to buy more stocks, which they used as collateral for more loans. Stock prices were soon bid up beyond any realistic value.

Brokers' loans during the boom grew from $2 billion to $8 billion. When the oversold market began to collapse, as it had to, banks were forced to call the brokers' loans as the value of their collateral dissolved. The brokers couldn't pay and went into insolvency, taking the banks with them.

Thus the Great Depression no one has been able to forget was presented to the American people by the same influential banking and brokerage houses who gave them the private-interest-oriented Aldrich plan, alias the Federal Reserve System.

A function of the FDIC, less known than its supposed protection of depositors from loss in the event of a run on banks, is its examining authority. Auditors of the FDIC regularly examine the books and management practices of banks which it insures. In the case of national banks and state banks which are members of the Federal Reserve System, the FDIC receives reports of audits conducted by the Comptroller of Currency and the Federal Reserve Board.

While these audits have the laudable effect of reducing embezzlement and mismanagement of funds, they have been accused also of hampering the growth of small business and/or farming in many communities since the main purpose of examiners' audits is to assure that the bank is operated for the *bank's* benefit, not necessarily for public or community benefit.

A loan to someone who wants to manufacture a poorly produced and misrepresented product will be adjudged "good" if the borrower has put up sufficient collateral. On the other hand, FDIC examiners may come down hard on a bank which has lent money for the establishment of businesses which are needed in the community or which will provide significant employment, simply because they feel inadequate collateral has been provided.

Knowing this, banks are often reluctant to make loans which would benefit a community.

Discouraging as this situation may be, it is nothing compared with the loss and disappointment to be faced by millions of Americans who have been led by the government to believe that their deposits are safe in the event there's ever a run on banks similar to the one we previously experienced.

FDIC protection? Don't bank on it.

The depositors who've placed their faith and hard-earned savings in America's thousands of savings banks would hardly fare better. According to the Federal Home Loan Bank Board *Journal,* the $194.5 billion 1973 deposits insured by the Federal Savings and Loan Insurance Corporation (the FDIC of savings-and-loan banking) are covered by a reserve of only $3.1 billion—about 1.6 per cent.

The FDIC and FSLIC were created to give bank

depositors a feeling of security, but should any one of a number of possible circumstances produce widespread withdrawals bringing about bank failures, "insured" depositors' claims could only be paid with almost worthless paper currency.

5

Whatever Happened to the $1.00 Cup of Coffee?

An American who starts work at 18 and who must live with a 5.5 per cent annual inflation rate will see prices double before he is thirty-one. And he will see prices double a third time before his fifty-seventh birthday. When he reaches seventy, he will have to pay sixteen times as much for whatever he buys as he did when he started out. His dollar will have shrunk to $.06¼, or by 93.75.

At age seventy-six he will have to pay thirty-two times as much in dollars and cents as he did when he took his first job. He would have to pay $1.60 for a pack of chewing gum and $4.80 for a cup of coffee.

Robert A. Hendrickson, Economist,
The Future of Money, 1970

During 1975 Robert Hendrickson's young worker, described above—and most other Americans—would look back on the late 1960's 5.5 per cent inflation rate as a boon of the "good old days." The 12 per cent inflation rate of late 1974 would double prices within a mere six years and raise the price of a cup of coffee to well over $1.00 before the year 2000.

University of Chicago Professor Milton Friedman is one of a growing body of economists who expect inflation to worsen, perhaps "rising to 14 per cent by 1976 and even faster in later years. The policies we follow," he says, "lead to a ratcheting up of inflation."

As early as May 1974, with inflation up to 8.3 per cent, Federal Reserve Chairman Arthur Burns broke ranks with other Nixon administration officials when he warned, "The gravity of our current inflationary problem can hardly be overestimated. If past experience is any guide, the future of our country is in jeopardy."

By mid-1974 many individuals, feeling dazed and helpless as though they had been attacked by a mugger, shook their heads and asked themselves, "What happened?" Hadn't the President promised economic law and order which would protect them from just such losses?

"When this Administration took office nine months ago," President Nixon told the American people in an address to the nation on October 17, 1969, "we decided that we were going to stop talking about higher prices and that we were going to start doing something about them. We are curing the causes of the rising cost of living."

On that same day in 1969 the President stated that his Administration was not "considering putting the government into the business of telling the working man how much he should charge for his services or how much the businessman should charge for his goods. . . . What we are going to do is based upon total realism."

In August of 1971, less than two years after he disavowed the possibility of a controlled economy, the President announced the establishment of wage and price controls more stringent than any our nation had experienced since World War II.

Where had this inflation come from? What happened? Why?

During early 1974, as inflation edged beyond the 5 per cent mark, economists, government agencies, and the news media were explaining inflation in the terms of Economics 101. There are, we were told, two basic types of inflation.

One, *demand inflation,* results when an oversupply of money bids up prices on a limited quantity of goods. If you go into your local car dealer to buy a new model and his business is booming because people in the community have lots of dollars to pay for cars, he'll be able to get a higher price for what he has to sell.

If business is slow for any reason, you'll be able to get a sizable discount, since no one is bidding against you to obtain the car.

To use the example in the Council of Economic Advisers' information booklet on inflation, if, on the second day of a cattle auction, bidders are each given an additional hundred dollars, they will use the extra money to bid prices higher than on the first day, even though the same number of steers were sold on the second day as on the first.

The cattle supply was the same both days, but the *price* went up on the second day because people had more money.

The second traditional type of inflation, *cost-push inflation,* begins either with business or labor, depending on whether the explainer happens to be affiliated with business or with labor.

In labor's model, business raises prices which affect the cost of living. Because the cost of living has risen, labor then must contract for higher wages to "stay even." Business then raises prices to compensate for higher labor costs. Continuing rounds of labor and price increases push prices higher and higher. In business' version of the cost-push cycle, prices initially rise only to compensate for increased labor costs. In any event, continuing rounds of labor and price increases push prices higher and higher.

In many respects, an increased money supply ignites both types of inflation. Easy money means customers have the extra dollars to bid up prices. And prices which have been bid up by people with plenty of money touch off cost-of-living increases which motivate labor to ask for higher wages.

If left alone, which is seldom, a free economy tends to dampen inflation-deflation cycles, resulting in a more or less even economy with only a modest (around 3 or 4 per cent) inflation rate.

Many noted economists, while admitting that demand inflation and cost-push inflation are both factors in our current crisis, state that government spending beyond income is the *primary* cause of our present inflationary spiral.

When a government spends more than it earns through taxes and other sources it is forced into *deficit spending*. The government is able to spend dollars it doesn't have by obtaining more money through a procedure whereby the Federal Reserve creates additional dollars in the form of government securities which banks "buy," thus lending the money back to the government (as explained previously in Chapter 3 "The Case Against The Federal Reserve.")

Our current inflationary fever has been incubating in the economy for more than ten years. According to the 1973 annual report of the Council of Economic Advisers, the money supply in the United States grew 47 per cent, from $259 billion to $382 billion, during the 1964–68 Johnson administration. During that time, however, our productivity increase was only 22 per cent —almost exactly the "normal" 4 per cent yearly gain.

Over the Nixon administration years, 1969 through 1973, the money supply increased 49 per cent, from $382 billion to $571 billion. Nixon era productivity remained 22 per cent.

During 1975 President Ford and the Congress each proposed annual federal budgets that produced deficits which could be counted on to touch off heightened inflation. Admitting that unemployment and not inflation were his biggest concern, President Ford, as he signed the $28-billion federal tax cut on March 29, stated that "if Congress had accepted all my economic proposals, both for tax cuts and spending cuts, the estimated federal deficit for fiscal year 1976 would have been about $52 billion.

"This kind of deficit is far too high, but most of it was unavoidable and was brought about by mandatory federal payment programs already on the statute books, by increased unemployment compensation and reduced tax revenues due to the recession. . . .

"The tax cuts in the bill I have just signed will bring the estimated fiscal year 1976 deficit up to approximately $60 billion."

Dollars pumped into the economy by deficit spending raised prices on nearly everything consumers wanted to buy, just as extra money given to cattle buyers in our example elevated the price of each steer put up for sale.

The symptoms of inflation weren't strongly felt at home during the 1960s because the fixed exchange rates and investments overseas combined to "export" our inflation to other countries.

Fixed exchange rates required foreign central banks to exchange their own currencies at fixed rates for dollars presented to them—mostly by banks within their own borders. Regardless of how "watered" our currency became, international agreements required foreign central banks to give a fixed amount of their own money for them. Dollars which today were less valuable than yesterday still commanded the same price in foreign currency.

Secondly, American investors and corporations were buying up foreign corporations and property on such a grand scale that French President Charles de Gaulle protested more than once that Americans were "buying up European industry with dollars arbitrarily produced by printing presses in the United States."

Since in both cases inflationary dollars were leaving the country instead of competing for goods at home, there was only a limited extra money supply to drive up prices within the United States.

On August 15, 1971, with its gold reserves dangerously low ($11.6 billion), the United States announced that it would "temporarily" cease paying gold to foreign governments in exchange for dollars.

On December 18, 1971, the United States Government devalued the dollar by 7.89 per cent. On February 12, 1973, the dollar was further devalued by 11 per cent.

Finally, the elimination of fixed exchange rates in 1973 ended our exportation of inflation. The honeymoon was over.

Ten years of government overspending came home to feed on the incomes and savings of the American people.

Was deficit spending really all that inflationary? What

about soaring Middle East oil prices? What about the 1972 Russian grain deal? What about U.S. crop failures? Were these too, not major contributors to our increasing inflation rate? Contributors, yes. Major, no.

Although fuel costs are seen as well as felt at every stop at the service station and petroleum costs figure in a wide range of products, oil price hikes in themselves would be hard put to account for even a two per cent rise in our cost of living during normal times.

Writing in the July 27, 1974, issue of *Saturday Review/World,* economist Sidney E. Rolfe pointed out:

> These elements, crop failures, Soviet wheat purchases and the soaring prices of grain, are important but have been, at most, marginal contributors [to inflation] or, in the case of oil, very late comers.
>
> Had there been no endemic inflation, the shortages might have raised prices as a whole one or two per cent. Putting it differently, they converted a 10 per cent inflation into perhaps a 12 per cent inflation.

Many economists agree that the Russian wheat deal and crop reverses would be little more than ripples on somewhat choppy economic waters if the Johnson and Nixon administrations had not deficit-spent America into near bankruptcy.

The Johnson administration, unable to tax the American people additionally to support an unpopular war in Vietnam, resorted to multibillion dollar deficit spending to finance its costs. The social programs of the "Great Society" added to the toll. Between 1965 and 1968 the Johnson administration increased federal spending by

$60 billion, *without* raising taxes to make up for the increase.

While there are no taped White House conversations about it, there is little doubt in the minds of astute political observers that prior to the 1972 election the Nixon administration embarked upon a policy of easy money to assure a booming economy and re-election when voters went to the polls. Again, the "creation" of money through deficit spending added to the inflationary tide.

The $305.4 billion fiscal 1976 budget left on the desk of President Ford when Richard Nixon vacated the White House was the largest federal budget in our entire history. It included a $9.4 billion deficit which hinged precariously on a $25 billion increase in revenue —which was all but eliminated by the late 1974 downturn in the economy.

Yet that deficit appears small when measured against the projections President Ford outlined in presenting his budget for 1975–76. Anticipating government expenditures of $349.4 billion against predicted revenues of $297.5 billion, the President thus presented the nation with a planned record peace-time deficit of $51.9 billion.

Within weeks, actions by the Congress clearly indicated that even that whopping deficit was woefully underestimated. Continued loss of tax revenues due to high unemployment rates, plus increased government spending for emergency economic proposals, will push the deficit much higher, perhaps to $100 billion.

To at least partially absolve the framers of the budget, it must be admitted that the federal budget is now largely out of control, that American inflation is now feeding upon itself, and that there is little that anyone can do to turn the economy around.

If federal spending is effectively reduced, mass unemployment will be the result. If a "full employment" budget is attempted, it can be the straw that tips the economic balance toward runaway inflation. As one government official told me, "It's like fighting two dragons; the minute you turn to fight one, the other is at your back."

During late 1974 the national debt surpassed $490 billion: $190 billion *more* than federal income.

At the end of 1974, interest on the national debt exceeded $32 billion.

Of the federal budget for fiscal 1976, about three quarters—more than $260 billion—is "uncontrollable" spending: expenditures which are obligatory under present law.

On February 5, 1975, Arizona Senator Barry Goldwater, stated, "I can see nothing but complete disaster in President Ford's $349 billion budget. I would like to support the President, but I don't believe the nation's economy could stand this kind of attack on its solvency.

"If we become politically realistic and understand that the Democrats will probably add a national health bill which could cost from $20 to $70 billion and then add an enlarged tax reduction plus other spending we are looking at a deficit this year of between $70 and $100 billion.

"I seriously question where the money will come from. The total debt of this country, including federal debt, state debt, local debt, and our own personal debts is more money than we have. So it gets to be rather simple arithmetic. The country, if it continues the spending that it is now engaged in, is going to have to print some more money. And this is precisely the reason we are in the trouble we are in now."

Payments to Individuals: $135.5 Billion. The largest single category of federal expenditure comprises government-financed programs that put money into the hands of people who qualify. This outlay accounted for 44 per cent of the 1974 budget—more than $135 billion. It includes payments for veterans' benefits, military and civil service retirement pay, Medicare ($14 billion), Medicaid, welfare payments, payments to retired railroad workers and disabled coal miners, unemployment benefits, food stamps, housing subsidies, and Social Security ($64 billion).

Farm Price Supports: $900 Million. The 1974 budget included $900 million for farm price supports, but actual costs for the program are expected to total more than that when final figures for the year are in. Total expenditures under the program are affected by foreign and domestic markets, prices at harvest time, and the amount of crops which are being supported.

United States Postal Service: $2 Billion. The Postal Service is still losing money despite postage rate increases. Increased operating costs resulting from inflation are expected to push the deficit which the U. S. Treasury must make up to around $2 billion, $400 million more than originally provided for.

States, Counties, Towns, and Cities: $8 Billion. The Nixon administration's revenue-sharing program obligated more than $8 billion to states and communities during fiscal 1974. This amount is almost impossible to reduce, since recipients have been told to count on it in preparing their budgets.

According to Office of Management and Budget director Roy Ash, 1974 "uncontrollables" added up to 75 per cent of the entire budget; of the remainder, all but $26 billion were allocated to defense. Congress can be expected to take a few tentative swipes at the proposed $95-billion defense budget, but the amount that can be realistically cut, or which would even be allowed by the politically powerful defense industry, is insignificant.

In summing up what he believes to be the three key elements of economic management which might lead to some measure of control over the United States' inflationary crisis, Council of Economic Advisers chairman Alan Greenspan replies, "The budget, the budget, and the budget."

No one denies the imperative need for major reductions in federal spending if inflation is to be prevented from soaring even higher, but nobody wants to take the political rap for doing the cutting.

House Speaker Carl Albert, when asked in November 1974 if he planned to lead his reinforced Democratic congressional majority in formulating an economic recovery plan, responded with a two-word reply: "Who, me?"

When the Democrats did reveal their plans, the message was clear: *more* government spending, not less, would be their approach to reviving the flagging economy. They favored new spending programs, primarily to create emergency public jobs or extend unemployment compensation benefits; acceleration of public works projects and other federally financed programs; tax cuts and tax rebates—in other words, a larger federal budget, smaller revenues, and a higher deficit, to be financed by an easing of the Federal Reserve's monetary policy.

The most realistic appraisal of America's chances of

avoiding runaway inflation or massive depression or both in the near future was voiced during late 1974 by Jodey T. Allen, director of policy studies at Mathematica, Inc., a "think tank" composed of economic consultants. Allen warned: There is no currently known way in theory or in fact to fight inflation and depression simultaneously."

Whatever measures are taken by the transitory experts in Washington, the choices will have to be made from a potentially violent herd of sacred cows. Things are going to get a lot worse before they can get better.

6

Who's Afraid of the CPI?

As inflation gathers momentum, rising prices rob people of a yardstick for measuring their demands and supplies, their consumption, savings, and investments. It creates deep-seated unrest in all relationships, from those between citizens and government to those between husband and wife.
Gunnar Myrdal, Economist, Stockholm University

For many years people thought of the consumer price index (CPI), sometimes called the cost of living index, as a relatively obscure statistic, far removed from their own lives and of interest mainly to theoretical economists and ivory-tower professors.

Today, if it were printed in a small "box" at the top of a daily newspaper's front page, each day's CPI would probably be noted and considered and its import analyzed before the weather forecast was checked or headlines read.

The difference between yesterday and today is that the sleeping CPI has awakened with a voracious appetite and is consuming the assets and savings of Americans like a swarm of locusts devouring a field of crops.

One fact about the CPI which few consider is that

even though an inflation rate may remain constant, its effect on the cost of living is compounded each year.

At a 7 per cent CPI increase (which the United States last saw in August 1973), an item priced in a given year at $100 will cost $107 twelve months later—7 per cent more than its original price.

At a continuing inflation rate of 7 per cent per year, the cost of the item will rise 14.49 per cent the second year compared to its original $100 cost two years before.

The third year, with the inflation rate still at 7 per cent, the cost of the item rises 22.5 per cent compared to its original price.

What is happening within the economy now however is far more damaging. The *rate of increase* in the cost of living is accelerating at a rate which is likely to be irreversible without a severe depression.

The following table illustrates how the rate of inflation has more than doubled in the United States during two thirds of 1973 and all of 1974:

1973	PER CENT CHANGE FROM PREVIOUS TWELVE MONTHS
May	+ 5.5
June	+ 5.9
July	+ 5.7
August	+ 7.5
September	+ 7.4
October	+ 7.9
November	+ 8.4
December	+ 8.8
1974	
January	+ 9.4
February	+10.0

1974	PER CENT CHANGE FROM PREVIOUS TWELVE MONTHS
March	+10.2
April	+10.2
May	+10.2
June	+11.0
July	+11.5
August	+11.0
September	+12.0
October	+12.0
November	+12.1
December	+12.2

With the CPI doubling in less than two years, anyone in their right mind would be afraid of the CPI.

The CPI, incidentally, came into being during World War I when living cost increases made some kind of index necessary for wartime wage negotiations. Thus in 1917 the CPI became the basis for labor contracts tied to the cost of living. Today such contracts cover millions of U.S. workers, and every inch of upward movement in the CPI raises the cost of many items which Americans buy every day. Manufacturers' increased costs are passed along to consumers in the form of higher prices—which raise the CPI, causing workers to be granted still higher wages.

The CPI is officially published in the monthly *Consumer Price Index for Urban Wage Earners and Clerical Workers* of the Department of Labor, Bureau of Labor Statistics. Price surveyors obtain costs by making personal visits to 18,000 stores. Monthly rental rates are obtained by mail from 40,000 tenants. In all, the CPI includes prices on items and services which people buy and pay for every day.

Prices are sampled in fifty-six large metropolitan areas and smaller cities like Cedar Rapids, Iowa; Anchorage, Alaska; Klamath Falls, Oregon; and Vicksburg, Mississippi.

Since 1971 the base period for the CPI has been 1967, with the CPI for that year being rated at 100. Looking at the CPI, it's easy for one to see that the cost of living has moved upward, without once retreating, each year for the past sixteen years:

1960	88.7
1961	89.6
1962	90.6
1963	91.7
1964	92.9
1965	94.5
1966	97.2
1967	100.0
1968	104.2
1969	109.8
1970	116.3
1971	121.3
1972	125.3
1973	133.1
1974	147.7
1975 (to Oct.)	164.6

Even in the best of years, nothing stays the same. It took only five years for the CPI to rise from 1970's 116.3 to 1974's 147.7. Even if the CPI increases at no more than its January 1975 rate, it will take $2.00 five years from now to buy what you can purchase with $1.00 today. The "price" of the item will not have gone up; the "value" of the dollar will just be half of what it is today.

If you were to buy the same item with the "real money" of gold or silver a year from now, its "price" would probably be the same, or even less, than it was during 1974 or 1975.

The economic storm warnings displayed by the soaring CPI are twofold:

Each day the buying power of the dollar is *less* than it was the day before.

Each day the rate of decrease in the dollar's buying power is *greater* than it was the day before.

On July 24, 1974, in his last major speech before resigning the presidency, Richard Nixon told Americans they really weren't so badly off after all. "Painful as our own inflation is," he said, "it is less than that of France, of Italy, of Great Britain, of Japan, and less than that of most of the industrial nations of the world."

That was bad news rather than good news, since the effect of international CPI increases turns up the fire under our own CPI.

In Britain the 1974 inflation rate was 15.9 and rising; in France it was 16.0 and rising; in Canada, 11.0 and rising; in Japan it was 23.2 and rising; in Portugal 26.6 and rising. The inflation rate in West Germany was 7.2 at the close of 1974. West Germany's inflation rate was the lowest of any industrialized nation, yet it was considerably above the rate which many U.S. economists generally agree would be "highly damaging" to the American economy.

There is little chance that any responsible economist will declare that the United States cost of living can remain untouched by rampant inflation in nations which supply many of the raw materials and products used in great quantity by the American economy.

There are several additional indexes which have to be mentioned because they provide further accuracy in charting the decline and fall of the American dollar.

One of these is the wholesale price index (WPI), which is based on the wholesale prices of a wide range of industrial, agricultural, and consumer goods. Like the CPI, the WPI takes 1967 as its base year, assigning a value of 100 for the WPI of that year.

During the last quarter of 1974 the Labor Department, which puts together the WPI, reported it registered its second highest rise in twenty-seven years.

The WPI for August 1974 rose to 167.4, meaning that it cost $167.40 at wholesale to buy goods which cost $100 in 1967. Since wholesale prices are passed along to consumers, a rising WPI pulls the CPI along after it.

The gross national product (GNP) is another measure used in defining the state of the economy. The GNP is the government's over-all index of the nation's total output of goods and services. It also includes the value of output produced outside the United States in facilities owned by Americans. Automobiles produced in Europe, for example, by Ford or General Motors are counted as part of America's GNP.

Although not universally accepted, the GNP is used as an indicator to establish the occurrence of a recession. According to most economists, a recession exists whenever there are two consecutive quarters' decline in the GNP. During 1974 the GNP dropped at an annual rate of 7 per cent the first quarter, 1.6 per cent the second, 0.0 the third quarter, and 0.0 the fourth quarter.

Economists, of course, more readily accept the GNP's message than do politicians. As early as October 1974, Federal Reserve Board chairman Arthur Burns told the Joint Congressional Economic Committee that the nation was in a recession. The same week President

Ford told a news conference that "I do not think the United States is in a recession."

The Dow Jones industrial average is the best-known and most closely followed of the several stock market indicators. It includes some thirty stocks which are America's most solid corporations, such as General Motors, United States Steel, American Telephone & Telegraph, and Eastman Kodak.

Using the Dow Jones average to index day-to-day stock market conditions may be like surveying residents of Beverly Hills, California, or Darien, Connecticut, to determine the living conditions of the United States population. Even so, the Dow-Jones has something to tell us about the failing health of the American economy.

Between January 11, 1973, and October 4, 1974, the Dow Jones fell from a high of 1,051.70 to 584, almost exactly where it was fourteen years before, in October of 1962. Take away the effect of inflation, though, and the "real" Dow Jones stood at 496.5, nearly 100 points *below* its October 1974 reading.

The more you correct for inflation, the worse the Dow Jones looks. Using the 1967 CPI as a base year, our sample 1974 584 Dow Jones average would be 389, wiping out all market gains since January 17, 1955.

Taking 1957 as a base, the Dow Jones would stand at 334, about where it was on July 1, 1954.

Taking 1947 as a base, the Dow Jones would fall to 214, not terribly far from where it was toward the end of the so-called Great Depression.

It doesn't take a very long look at the hard facts to realize there's good reason to be afraid of the CPI—and the WPI—and the GNP—and, just for good measure, the Dow Jones industrial average.

7

A Touch of Insanity

Millions of people justifiably feel that the economy is cheating them of the rewards of hard work and thrift. A few more years of skyrocketing prices which wipe out much of the middle class and reduce some Americans to eating dogfood could well cause many voters to question whether a system so fundamentally flawed can endure. Public demoralization is being vastly increased by a gnawing fear that no one knows how to stop inflation in a modern democratic capitalist economy.

Time magazine, July 29, 1974

The American system isn't "so fundamentally flawed" as it is the victim of pilot error. When the economy of the country crashes, the ultimate finding will surely be that it was navigated into harm's way by a series of inept captains and a gang of hijackers masquerading as bankers and businessmen.

If it didn't hurt so much, you could almost laugh—an insane comedy of errors dragging a great nation like the United States to the brink of bankruptcy, robbing its citizens of control over their lives, and leaving the few remaining rich in control of a country at the edge of ruin. But the tragedy strikes too close to home—and it won't be over when the last-act curtain descends.

For many years the government has resorted to deficit spending, the creation of new "printing-press" currency unbacked by gold, to achieve political ends.

President Johnson knew the American people could never be sold on increased taxes to pay for the unpopular Vietnam war, so his Administration resorted to billions in deficit spending. He realized too that it was not possible to pay for the social programs of his Great Society by increasing government revenue, so he again chose to jack up the national debt.

When unemployment and the menace of recession threatened to give voices to President Nixon's "silent majority" on the eve of the 1972 presidential election, he too used printing-press money to give the economy a reviving shot in the arm that would last long enough for him to be re-elected.

In 1972 President Nixon bought temporary prosperity with paper dollars. Since then, additional increases in the money supply, coupled with sales of Treasury gold during the early months of 1975, have reduced the backing of our currency even further.

Not only have successive administrations reduced the ratio of gold to dollars through excessive increases in the paper money supply, but they have allowed U.S. gold reserves to dwindle to a shadow of the amount needed to maintain economic stability.

During 1974 there were approximately 943 paper dollars in circulation for each ounce of gold in the U. S. Treasury, that is, gold backing of less than 5 per cent for American currency. While the number of paper dollars in circulation increases, the amount of our gold reserves declines.

YEAR	U.S. GOLD RESESRVES MILLIONS OF TROY OUNCES
1949	701
1950	651
1960	509
1965	394
1968	296
1974	276
1975	274

Not only has the value of our currency been debased, but the American economy has been allowed—even encouraged—to become less and less productive. Twenty-five years ago there were 22 million people doing productive work, compared to some 14 million officials and clerks. Today the number of productive workers has fallen to 18 million, but the number of non-productive workers has grown to 21 million.

During World War II, with more than 12 million men and women in uniform, there were 139 three- and four-star generals and admirals. Today, with only 2 million in uniform, there are 190.

Is this perhaps because military administrators are less costly than civilian administrators might be on the rolls of the Defense Department? If it is, how do you account for this: in 1969 there were 35 Defense Department civilian employees for every 100 military. Today there are 42 Defense Department employees for every 100 people in uniform.

Today one sixth of the civilian labor force is in government: supervising, controlling, policing, watching over, and manipulating the rest of the population, "producing" mainly regulations, forms, and paperwork.

From about 5 million in 1955, the number of self-employed persons in the United States has declined to barely a million today.

Wisconsin's Senator William Proxmire has repeatedly pointed out that "by closing the gap between the low actual performance and the potential performance of the economy we could generate $60 billion a year in additional growth which private citizens and governments at all levels could use to meet the nation's unmet needs."

Many of America's prime needs are not being met because of federal favoritism which encourages inefficiency and limits output in many areas of the gross national product. This favoritism reduces competition and provides hidden "welfare payments" to large, politically powerful industries.

Airlines: The Civil Aeronautics Board (CAB) protects air carriers from route and price competition and removes incentives for them to operate on the most efficient basis. In two of the nation's largest states, California and Texas, intrastate carriers not subject to CAB regulations provide service between cities like Los Angeles and San Francisco, and Houston and Dallas, at rates which are about half those charged by CAB-regulated interstate carriers.

The CAB recently refused the application of Laker Airways to fly passengers from New York to London at about one third the regular "economy" fare of CAB certified carriers.

In November 1974 the CAB issued guidelines that would put a "floor" under charter airlines' fares to Europe, a decision that will lead to a 35 per cent rate increase during 1975.

Sea Transportation: The Jones Act requires that all cargo moving by sea between United States ports be carried only on U.S.-flag ships. Depending on distances, this requirement can raise the retail cost of some goods as much as 20 per cent. It especially increases living costs in Hawaii and Alaska. Privately, United States oilmen say that if non-U.S. tankers could be utilized, it might well be economically feasible to use the Northwest Passage to move oil from Alaska's North Slope instead of building costly pipelines.

Trucking: The Interstate Commerce Commission (ICC) has established cartel-like tariffs which protect all but the most inefficient operators. Trucking companies are prohibited from carrying goods on "backhauls" at rates which would cover costs for the service. In many cases, truckers must return vehicles to their home bases empty rather than find their own loads at rates which they would happily—and profitably—accept.

Nearly 40 per cent of ICC-regulated carriers are limited to carrying one commodity, even though their equipment is suited to transporting more than one type of cargo.

In its November 4, 1974, issue, *Time* magazine reported that "during the height of the gasoline shortage, Consolidated Freightways was denied use of interstate highways to points south of Minneapolis, preventing a mileage decrease (for certain shipments) of 48 per cent."

When the shipment of chickens by truck was recently deregulated, the truck rates on frozen and fresh chickens declined by more than 30 per cent.

ICC protection also keeps interstate household-goods moving rates artificially high, so that families changing residence from one state to another are forced to pay amounts set as steep as large trucker lobbyists were able to get them.

A 1971 study by the Brookings Institution in Washington, D.C., determined that the existence of the Interstate Commerce Commission created an implicit "tax" on the economy of $5 billion or more.

Labor: The Davis-Bacon Act of 1930 stipulates that construction workers on projects using federal funds must be paid the "prevailing local wage." In practice, the "prevailing local wage" is often determined by the U. S. Labor Department to be the highest union scale paid anywhere within a hundred miles of the job site. The so-called "prevailing wages" paid on government-financed projects act to jack up the floor under a broad spectrum of labor costs in the area.

Foreign Trade: The "Buy America Act" sets federal procurement preferences which require the United States Government to buy many items from domestic manufacturers which it could often purchase at savings of up to 50 per cent from foreign sources.

Agriculture: Hundreds of Agriculture Department "marketing orders" artificially maintain high prices for many food items through restrictive size and grade requirements. Other restrictions on food imports—low-priced New Zealand and Australian beef, for example—cost consumers needless dollars every time they go to the supermarket.

According to Federal Trade Commission chairman Lewis A. Engman, "Most regulated industries have become federal protectorates, living in the cozy world of cost-plus, safely protected from the ugly specters of competition, efficiency, and innovation.

"Our airlines, our truckers, our railroads, our electronic media, and countless others are on the dole. We get irate about welfare fraud, but our complex systems of hidden regulatory subsidies make welfare fraud look like petty larceny."

In many cases regulatory agencies and government

advisory groups are "stacked" with members who have the best interests of industry, not the people, at heart.

Not long ago, the ICC created the Tariff Users (i.e., shippers) Advisory Commitee. It appointed seven trucking industry representatives and four carrier representatives, but no shipper representative.

When the Civil Aeronautics Board Finance Advisory Committee was established, its first meeting was held at the New York City home office of the Chase Manhattan Bank under the chairmanship of a Chase Manhattan vice president. The committee excluded press and public from its meetings and made recommendations on the CAB's procedures, conduct, and method of compiling financial reports.

Would you care to guess who is principal creditor for five of the nine local service air carriers as well as a principal stockholder in both Eastern and Northwest Orient airlines? The Chase Manhattan Bank, of course.

Several years ago, when the Defense Department appointed the so-called "Blue-Ribbon Defense Panel" to "restore public confidence in the Department of Defense," nine of the panel's fifteen members were named from corporations which averaged more than $250 million annual sales each either in defense contracts or defense industry holdings.

The "impartial" research contractor for the Blue-Ribbon Panel was the Stanford Research Institute—which had just received $27 million in government contracts, including $2.5 million to study the feasibility of the ABM missile system. These were the advisers which then-Defense Secretary Melvin Laird said would bring the problems of the Defense Department "into fresh, objective, and uninvolved perspective."

In 1970 President Nixon created the National Industrial Pollution Control Council to "advise the President and the Council on Environmental Quality." Not one single member of an environmental, consumer, or conservation group was appointed to the newly created council. Its membership was made up exclusively of the top executives of the sixty-three biggest polluters in the United States—men from steel mills, oil refiners, utility companies, auto makers, paper manufacturers, chemical companies, and others.

Where does the government get data on which to base decisions which "regulate" and "control" the petroleum industry? From government geologists, petroleum experts and economists? You know better than that by now. It relies for its decisions on data almost completely provided by the oil industry lobby, the biased experts of the American Petroleum Institute.

You can hardly watch TV or listen to radio for more than a few minutes without being urged in a "public service" commercial to buy U. S. Savings Bonds. Yet how does the government invest its own money to gain maximum return and perhaps reduce taxes a bit?

Here's one way. The Department of the Treasury, as this is being written in 1975, has on deposit in the ten largest banks in the United States more than $1 billion in noninterest-bearing accounts. These favored banks—the Bank of America, First National City Bank, Chase Manhattan, and Continental Illinois, to name a few—are free to invest this money in any way they choose—and to keep the income.

This favoritism to big banks costs taxpayers $77 million a year which the Treasury could earn if the same billion dollars were placed in any one of a wide range of interest-bearing investments. The "missing" $77 million must be made up through direct tax payments.

Here's another way. Every time the Treasury Department decides to float a major bond issue, it meets with representatives of the giant banks and "negotiates" a rate of interest. Then the bond issue is opened for subscription, which is restricted to a limited number of big financial institutions. Every bond issue is oversubscribed because the "negotiated" interest rate is too high. The high rate not only profits bankers at taxpayers' expense, but it drives up other interest rates and draws money out of the available lending market.

For decades the government has overtaxed the average American to meet interest payments on the national debt which end up in the pockets of bankers who control the private banks which are stockholders in the Federal Reserve System.

The government is also engaging in the fiscal insanity of overtaxing hard-working individuals and companies which have no political influence to make up for tax exemption and tax deduction "welfare payments" to big business.

Economists testifying before the House-Senate Joint Economic Committee recently estimated that big business and the wealthy each year receive more than $77 billion through subsidies, tax loopholes, and other handouts.

The corporate percentage share of total federal revenues is maneuvered lower each year. In 1950 corporate income taxes provided 25 per cent of the government's annual revenues. In 1960 corporate income taxes provided only 23 per cent. By 1973 the corporate income tax share of that year's revenues had fallen to 16 per cent. Figures for 1974 will not be available until well into 1975, but conservative estimates place the corporate tax share of federal revenues for 1974 at no more than 12 per cent—about half the figure for 1960.

Growing numbers of giant corporations pay no income tax at all. Here are a few which paid not one cent of income tax for 1973:

COMPANY	1973 EARNINGS	1973 FEDERAL INCOME TAX PAID
Bankers Trust N.Y. Corp.	$ 51.7 million	0
Western Bancorp.	97.7 million	0
Consolidated Edison	203.3 million	0
American Electric Power	194.3 million	0
Freeport Minerals Co.	23.9 million	0
Texas Gulf, Inc.	67.4 million	0
Chemical New York Corp.	74.7 million	0

Additional figures from a 1974 study by the Congressional Joint Committee on Internal Revenue Taxation indicate that another twenty giant corporations, with profits surpassing $5.3 billion, paid 1973 income taxes at an effective rate of from 1 to 10 per cent.

Major U.S. petroleum companies which, incidentally, are now charging Americans the same $11 per barrel for crude oil as the Arabs, are particularly adept at avoiding taxes.

Exxon, the nation's largest petroleum corporation, paid 1973 taxes at an effective rate of 11.2 per cent on earnings of $2.98 billion. Mobil paid taxes at an effective rate of 5 per cent on earnings of $873 million, and Texaco paid 2.3 per cent on earnings of $1.32 billion.

None of the tax-avoidance practices followed by the major corporations we've cited is illegal; they've just managed to buy and influence politicians into writing laws and tax regulations for their benefit.

By every measure, wealth in the United States is being legislated, maneuvered, and taxed out of the savings and pocketbooks of average Americans and into the hands of a few.

In 1968, according to the Federal Trade Commission, the 100 largest corporations held a greater percentage of manufacturing assets in the U.S. than did the 200 largest corporations in 1950. In 1968 the 200 largest manufacturing corporations controlled a share of corporate assets equal to that held by the largest 1,000 corporations in 1941.

During 1973 more than 100 individuals with incomes of $200,000 or more a year paid no federal income tax at all. A number of individuals with annual incomes exceeding $1 million paid no federal income tax at all.

Control of the American economy is devolving to smaller and smaller numbers of increasingly wealthy individuals and corporations whose political influence, often obtained through the use of lobbyists and through illegal political campaign contributions, creates tax loopholes which they regularly use to place their funds beyond the reach of tax collectors.

Wealthy individuals owning two or three homes took income tax deductions for mortgage interest on every one of their houses, yet poor families whose incomes were too low to pay income tax received no "federal housing reimbursements" at all.

A handful of private banks and investment firms each year receive billions of dollars in payments on the national debt which they claim as stockholders of the Federal Reserve System.

The main cause of inflation, almost anyone will tell you, is excessive government spending—and whoever you listen to is quite ready to point out the culprit.

Former President Nixon: "Now, there was a very simple reason why your cost of living got out of hand. The blame for the spiral of wages and prices falls fundamentally on the past policies of your government."

Senator William Proxmire: "You have to realize that the Nixon administration has proposed a $35-billion increase in spending for 1974 over 1973, the biggest dollar increase in our history and one of the biggest percentage increases ever."

President Ford: "The biggest burden of guilt [for inflation] lies on the shoulders of the biggest spenders and the fact is that one political party has run Congress and held the nation's purse strings for the past twenty straight years. That party is the Democratic party."

The Washingon *Post:* "The Nixon administration has broken all previous records, producing both the first $200-billion budget and the first $300-billion one. The monetary policy, rather than being 'tight,' has been notoriously free and easy."

According to Nixon administration Council of Economic Advisers chairman Dr. Herbert Stein, consumers are to blame for inflation. "The people," he stated, "were reluctant to have a tax increase and gave in to the temptation to buy."

Regardless of what is said by the White House, by economists, or by politicians, the concentration of power in the hands of a few individuals and corporations which President Truman frequently referred to as "special interest" has gone too far for any anti-inflationary measures to be taken which will in the least threaten the interests of large corporations, powerful banks, or the wealthy.

The American people were promised by President Nixon that wage-and-price controls would not be imposed, only to be told by the same President less than a year later that he was instituting the most sweeping wage-and-price controls program seen in the United States since World War II.

The American people were hit on August 15, 1971, and again on February 12, 1973, with surprise dollar devaluations which substantially and suddenly reduced the purchasing power of their currency.

In 1968 the government announced that it would no longer redeem "silver certificates" for silver, and on August 15, 1971, President Nixon announced that the United States would "temporarily" stop exchanging gold to foreign governments in exchange for dollars.

It was as though the United States had written a check to a foreign government and then told it when it came to the Treasury to cash it, "We're sorry, but we have 'temporarily' stopped payment."

Despite the Nixon administration's assurance that the suspension of gold payments would be "temporary," pressure to resume the exchange of dollars for gold is mounting. Foreign governments resent being "stuck" with $130 billion in U.S. paper currency.

If the United States is to ever again honor its own currency at the Treasury Department's exchange window, it will have to devalue the dollar from its fictional value of $42.22 per ounce of gold to something near gold's actual value. This would mean a dollar devaluation of about 400 per cent, but it is a step which must be taken sooner or later.

The point I hope to make in this chapter is that we have little reason to believe the government can do anything very effective to head off continuing inflation. Many inflationary pressures are already "built in" to our economy by law, and the political expediency of getting elected "just one more time" motivates Congress to spend now and let tomorrow's voters pay later.

Even if Congress and the American people were dedicated to appreciably slowing inflation, say, to 5 per cent a year, our monetary decay has proceeded too far for recovery and the government is strait-jacketed by special interests which make it run for their comfort and convenience, not yours.

Now that the 1974 congressional elections are over with, here are two things that will take place during 1976 or 1977:

1. The government will further devalue the dollar by the biggest percentage ever, at least 35 per cent.
2. The government will prohibit U.S. citizens from transferring their assets out of the country.

The time has finally arrived for those who would weather the coming economic hurricane to look out for themselves and put their assets outside the reach of inflation by investing in the *long-term* appreciation of gold and silver, in some of the more stable, gold-backed, foreign currencies, and in almost any asset which is beyond the touch of insanity.

8

Boy, Have I Got a Stock for You!

> *While the Dow-Jones industrial average has declined somewhere between 35 and 40 per cent, I suspect that the average investor has seen his portfolio shrink by something closer to 60 to 80 per cent. In some cases the catastrophe has been a complete wipeout. It has pushed upon everyone the necessity to re-examine such appealing shibboleths as 'Equity securities are a hedge against inflation.' When inflation became the worst in our lifetime, equity investments went to hell: some hedge!*
>
> A. A. Sommer, Jr., Commissioner,
> Securities and Exchange Commission,
> September 1974

In spite of the fact that stocks are commonly referred to as "securities," the stock market offers individual investors little more security than a rigged gambling wheel in a casino located astride the San Andreas fault.

Investors' paper assets fade with each downward turn of corporate profits, and the fragile wealth of those who purchased "blue-chip" stocks for long-term gains has been almost wiped out by the 1973–74 inflationary recession. Already, the percentage losses of many supposedly solid stocks are edging close to their 1929 declines.

During the first nine months of 1974, 31 million stockholders lost more than $500 *billion*. The market drop of 1974 wasn't so dramatic as the overnight crash of 1929; today we are buying depression on the installment plan.

The dangers of inflation and recession aside, the stock market has never been a place where individual investors could count on being safe from tigers.

The stock market is susceptible to the whim of large institutional investors; it is a fertile field for manipulation, it is rife with tainted and incompetent advice, and it is so safe a sanctum for confidence men that it has been called the "playground of swindlers." No wonder smart individual investors are staying away in droves.

A few years ago, when a nationwide advertising campaign urged people to "take stock in America," 67 per cent of all trading on the New York Stock Exchange (NYSE) was done by individuals. Today only about 40 per cent of the trading is done by individuals; the remainder is done by institutions.

The preponderance of institutional trading threatens individual investors two ways. First, large investor institutions, such as universities and pension plans, tend to trade in blocks of ten thousand shares or more. They can send a particular stock tumbling if, for any reason, they decide to sell out.

"Critics of the [stock] market," points out Securities and Exchange Commission chairman Ray D. Garrett, Jr., "describe the modest investor who went to work with his portfolio in good shape only to find when he came home to dinner that his savings had been wiped out; not because anything happened to the company whose stock he held, nor to the industry or the economy, but because some pension fund decided to unload, which triggered other institutional sheep to follow—and the market had been shattered."

A second danger to individual investors is created whenever the holdings of large institutions leave only a relatively small percentage of a particular stock in the market. With only a few shares available for trading, a speculator with sufficient backing can maneuver the market on that stock up or down—to his profit and to small investors' loss.

The federal government in the last forty years made two major efforts to reduce fraud and manipulation in the market and to protect investors when brokers and dealers go bankrupt because of mismanagement or market losses. One of the peculiarities of the stock market is that, unlike real estate or gold or silver bullion where you can personally examine your purchase, you must place almost complete reliance on the representations of others with respect to the value of securities you buy. This condition once led to a wide range of abuses which the government attempted to check.

In the first place, in 1934 Congress created the Securities and Exchange Commission (SEC), to reduce fraud and manipulation of the market, mostly by requiring full disclosure of information regarding stock issues which must meet certain *disclosure* requirements in order to be registered with the SEC for sale by brokers and dealers.

Brokers and dealers must also be registered with the SEC and must conform in their business practices to standards prescribed by law and SEC regulations. (A *broker*, by the way, serves as the customer's *agent* in buying or selling securities *for* his customer. A *dealer* acts as *principal* and buys securities *from* and sells securities *to* his customer.)

SEC officials stress that "The Commission cannot deny stock registration nor otherwise bar securities from public sale whether or not the price or other terms of the securities is fair, or whether the issuing company even offers reasonable prospects of success. *These are factors which the investor must assess for himself.* Nor does stock registration guarantee the accuracy of the facts represented in the registration statement or prospectus."

A second effort to protect investors was made by the Congress in 1970 with the creation of the Securities Investor Protection Corporation (SIPC), a sort of FDIC of the brokerage industry.

Congress saw the need for SIPC when millions of investors lost their savings as the result of brokerage bankruptcies due to the 1968–70 recession. Investors' cash and securities in the possession of brokers and dealers was never recovered, and many stockholders were "frozen in place" while they watched their holdings decline in value because they were unable to sell.

SIPC can now ask courts to appoint trustees for failing or failed broker-dealers and can advance money to the trustees for payment to customers of bankrupt broker-dealers up to a maximum of $50,000 per customer. In 1971 SIPC paid out $476,000 to customers of failed broker-dealers. In 1972 it paid out $8.1 million, and in 1973 it paid out $202 million.

The somewhat parallel investor protection tracks of SIPC and the SEC meet at one crossroads of concern: of the ninety-four firms placed in liquidation during

1973, possible fraud and misconduct were contributing factors in fifty-five instances.

Fraud is a major and continuing concern of SEC chairman Garrett. "I realize," he says, "that people get tired of hearing SEC commissioners talk about fraud—we seem obsessed with the subject, like a Puritan preacher with sex and sin—but there is more of it than there ought to be."

There is ample opportunity for fraud in almost every facet of the market. "Old-boy" relationships born of Ivy League and prep school associations, plus widespread nepotism, tend to make Wall Street a private club where voices are seldom raised against the professional impropriety of members.

Indeed, the NYSE *Guidelines for Member Firms' Communications With The Public* states: "Books on investing authored by member firm personnel are also subject to Exchange standards and the Advertising Department will review manuscripts. . . . It is important to submit such material well in advance since more time is required for review, and corrections can be troublesome and costly if the publication process is in the later stages."

Assistant NYSE advertising director David Dennison confirms that, saying, "We do have to approve books on finance or Wall Street or investment written by partners, registered representatives, analysts, even an unregistered employee of a member firm—even if he did a novel about Wall Street."

Wall Street censorship over the writing of members and employees, "makes the Catholic Church's censorship amateurish," adds *Barron's* columnist Alan Abelson.

Wall Street is increasing pressure on the Securities

and Exchange Commission to concern itself more with the welfare of brokers and less with the protection of investors. Says SEC commissioner John R. Evans, "We are told that we should protect and promote the industry and increase our concern with making the industry more profitable, and we are given suggestions as to how this should be accomplished. We are urged to switch our focus from investor protection to industry protection. This request must be on the assumption that our actions to protect investors are not beneficial to the industry."

As it is, enforcement efforts of the SEC sustain much of the old-boy tradition of inside Wall Street. SEC officials informed me that "Most of the Commission's investigations are conducted privately, the facts being developed to the fullest extent possible through informal inquiry, interviewing of witnesses, examination of brokerage records and other documents, reviewing of trading data and by similar means."

Penalties, even for willful, continued, and major fraud, remain minimal. In many cases, fraud involving sums that would send less genteel thieves to prison is often dealt with by withdrawing a broker-dealer's registration—the "license" which allows him to do business.

But fraud and misrepresentation are not visited upon investors only by broker-dealers. Accountants, lawyers, and the managements of great and small corporations all seem tempted by easy pickings from the pockets of the innocent and uninformed.

Thirty minutes' perusal of the Securities and Exchange Commission's daily *SEC News Digest* is enough to ruin your whole day—but I wouldn't try to read it before going to bed either. Here are a few excerpts (italics within excerpts, mine):

SEC News Digest, July 16, 1974: "The Commission has revoked the broker-dealer registration of A. P. Montgomery & Co. Inc., of New York, suspended its president, Richard S. Friedman, from association with any broker-dealer, investment advisor or investment company *for a period of 180 days,* and barred Friedman from any such association in a nonsupervised capacity. After his suspension, Friedman may apply for permission to become so associated in a nonsupervisory capacity.

"The sanctions were based upon findings that *from February 1, 1972 to May 1, 1973,* the firm and Friedman violated antifraud and antimanipulative provisions of the securities act in transactions involving the common stocks of SaCom and Manchester Life and Casualty Management Corporation . . . artificially maintained the prices of those securities . . . created false and misleading appearance of the markets for them by entering into arrangements with persons engaged in the distribution of the securities . . . and made purchases and sales with a guaranteed profit agreements.

"The Commission also found that from January 1 through July, 1972, the firm and Friedman committed additional violations of the antifraud provisions, as well as violating credit extension and record-keeping provisions, in transactions involving short sales of the securities of the Adobe Corporation, Fidelity Financial Corporation, Forest Oil Corporation, Storage Technology Corporation and Tufto Corporation. The firm improperly extended credit in short sales to it, and falsified its records by recording short sales as long sales. . . .

"The Commission's order was issued under an offer

of settlement in which the firm and Friedman, without admitting or denying the charges against them in two administrative proceedings, consented to the findings and sanctions."

SEC News Digest, August 6, 1974: "The SEC announced that on August 8, the Federal court for the District of Columbia permanently enjoined Mattel, Inc., of Hawthorne, Calif., from violations of the antifraud and corporate reporting provisions of the securities laws. The Court also granted other relief. Mattel consented to the Court order without admitting or denying the allegations of the Commission's complaint.

"In its complaint the Commission alleged, among other things, that Mattel filed false and misleading quarterly reports with the Commission and issued false and misleading press releases stating that it was experiencing a substantial turnaround and had made profits for the first three quarters of its 1973 fiscal year ending February 3, 1973. . . . In fact, Mattel had experienced operating losses throughout the year. . . ."

SEC News Digest, May 24, 1974: "An order has been issued barring Sidney Frank Bahr, of Bethlehem, Pennsylvania, and Edwin A. Schrader, of Orefield, Pennsylvania, from association with any broker or dealer. According to the decision, Bahr and Schrader sold unregistered stock of International Resources, Inc., and made misrepresentations about the expected rise in its price, and International's financial condition and future prospects. It also found that Bahr made misstatements in connection with transactions in the stock of General Energy Corporation about the expected rise in its price, the listing of that stock on various exchanges, General's prospects, and the extent of its uranium holdings. Bahr and Schrader failed to appear at the hearings, and were deemed in default."

SEC News Digest, August 21, 1974: "The Commission has revoked the broker-dealer registration of Cenco Investors & Associates, Inc., of Grand Rapids, Mich., formerly known as C. E. Cook & Co., and barred its president, C. Eugene Cook, from association with any broker or dealer. After five years, however, Cook may apply to the Commission for permission to become so associated in a nonsupervisory capacity upon a showing of adequate supervision.

"The sanctions imposed were based upon the findings that from January 1971 to September 1973, the firm, aided and abetted by Cook, violated the antifraud provisions of the securities laws in securities transactions of numerous named companies in that they, among other things, misrepresented and failed to state material facts, made recommendations without reasonable basis, 'switched' customers into speculative securities, sold securities at excessive prices and effected transactions in customers' accounts without authorization. . . .

"The Commission's order was issued after an offer of settlement in which the firm and Cook, without admitting or denying the charges against them, consented to the findings and sanctions."

SEC News Digest, May 23, 1974: "An order has been issued barring Michael Hellerman, of Bayside, New York, from association with any broker-dealer, registered investment advisor or registered investment company. The sanction was based upon findings that from about May 1969 to February 1970, Hellerman violated registration and antifraud provisions of the securities laws in activities involving the common stock of Imperial Investment Corporation. Hellerman unlawfully sold unregistered Imperial stock, and engaged in a manipulative scheme designed to create and maintain an artificial market for that stock. Hellerman also made material misrepresentations about the existence of a bona fide independent market for Imperial stock, the source of the stock being offered and sold, and his participation in the manipulation.

"Hellerman consented to the findings and sanction without admitting or denying the charges against him."

SEC News Digest, July 2, 1974: "The New York Regional Office and the Division of Enforcement announced that on July 1 the Commission filed a complaint in the U. S. District Court for New York seeking to enjoin J. Hugh Liedtke, William C. Liedtke, Jr., and Choctaw Corporation of Houston, Texas from violations of the antifraud provisions of the securities laws. The complaint alleges that J. Hugh Liedtke and William C. Liedtke, Jr., chairman and president of Penzoil Company, respectively, caused Choctaw Corporation to buy 125,000 shares of Penzoil common stock while they possessed knowledge of the impending spin-off of United Gas Company, a Penzoil subsidiary, and a proposed dividend of one million shares of preferred stock to be paid by United Gas and Penzoil, before that material information was made public. The defendants have consented, without admitting or denying the allegations, to a permanent injunction and have agreed to pay $108,125 into a trust for the benefit of those persons who sold Penzoil stock to the Choctaw Corporation from December 21, 1973 to February 20, 1974."

The above are only a few instances of fraud, misrepresentation, and use of "insider" information which appear by the hundreds like a daily litany of deceit on the pages of the *SEC News Digest.*

"Decisions in Administrative Proceedings," in which investigations resulting in sanctions are announced, and "Court Enforcement Actions," in which court orders are listed, can be found in the weekly *SEC Docket*. If you have a taste for horror stories you can subscribe to either from the Securities and Exchange Commission. The *SEC News Digest* is $35.45 per year and the *SEC Docket* is $21.35.

SEC commissioner Sommer is one of several who feel that stronger penalties than mere revocation of broker-dealer registration are needed, to materially reduce the mugging of investors on the dark corners of Wall Street:

> We must convince federal district attorneys and state prosecutors that these [stock market frauds] are serious crimes that deserve serious punishment, that it is an incredible inequity and a profound unfairness to society, to send a man to jail for ten years for armed robbery when he steals a few hundred dollars, while a white-collar executive bilks the public out of millions and gets either probation or a few months in jail . . .
>
> Despite our disclosure system and regulatory efforts, billions of dollars are frittered away in this country every year, not in honest speculative ventures that don't turn out well but in outright frauds; oil schemes where the proceeds go not into drilling, but into Cadillacs and mansions for promoters; real estate deals that offer the traditional acreage under the ocean; interest in mines that have lain dormant for years and will continue to lie dormant because they are simply no good. . . .
>
> Trusting Americans, despite all the Commission's forty years of endeavor . . . are bilked out of their dreams, their hopes, their savings, their comforts and their security.

Unfortunately, the SEC and many honest brokers are too often deceived by dishonest corporate managements who, with and without the collusion of unethical accountants and attorneys, manage to secure registration for near-worthless stocks.

The recent and major Equity Funding case is an example of Wall Street's "best intentions," and the SEC's best efforts, failing to prevent thousands of investors from losing millions of dollars in a major white-collar fraud.

From 1967 through 1969 the common stock of Equity Funding Corporation of America was one of the glamour issues on Wall Street. From a 1967 low of 7.50 it soared to 81.00 a share in 1969. Though it declined to the 40s during 1973, it remained a favorite with investment advisers and market pros who managed the portfolios of institutional investors. They liked an Equity Funding subsidiary's success in selling a customer mutual-fund shares, which were then used as collateral for loans to finance insurance purchases.

During the first three quarters of 1972 Equity Funding Life Insurance Company posted sales of $1.8 billion, placing it among the top ten of all life insurers.

The bubble burst when investigators found that $10.5 of the $14.5 million in premiums which Equity Funding Life claimed for 1972 were nonexistent.

During the investigation former employees reported working nights at "fraud parties" making up false policies and tampering with the company's books to fool auditors. Equity Funding Life then followed a common practice of cash-short insurance companies and sold the policies to other insurers to obtain operating capital.

According to California chief deputy insurance commissioner Lawrence C. Baker, Jr., "Only about 40,000 of the 100,000 policies reported by Equity Life actually existed." Fred A. Mauck, Illinois state insurance director, states that, "There was no trace of the $20 million in negotiable bonds which Equity Life claimed as assets."

The Equity Funding case, in 1975, has yet to be concluded. Illinois insurance director Mauck reports, "The situation for policy holders looks relatively good, although it's not good for shareholders and creditors."

In the case of Equity Funding, the corporation's stock was recommended to investors by advisers of virtually every major brokerage house on Wall Street. It was described as "another IBM," "another Xerox," and "another Polaroid" by experienced analysts, who took the company's word for its assets, sales, profits, and prospects.

When asked how the Securities and Exchange Commission can "let Equity Funding happen?" SEC commissioner Sommer said:

> The Commission simply does not have the statutory mandate or the people capacity to discern frauds as they develop. The Commission's principal statutory mandate, other than regulation of the securities industry . . . is to see to it that adequate disclosure is made in connection with distributions of securities, and this mandate does not particularly equip the SEC to perform the sort of function that many think is imposed upon it: the detection of fraud in its incipiency.
>
> The Equity Funding filings with the Commission and the New York Stock Exchange didn't tell the most important fact: that over two billion dollars of alleged insurance didn't exist, that over $140,000,000 of the assets on the books were just that—on the books and nowhere else. The filings of

another glamour company omitted a most important fact: that the heads of the company were phonying the books to soup up earnings.

Who can you trust in the market? Several years ago Norman Poser, a sharp young SEC attorney, decided to look into the effect of publicity on the rise and fall of common stock. One of the fast-moving stocks that caught Poser's eye was Technical Animations, Inc., which had soared briefly to 15½ before dropping to 4½.

Poser visited the broker who was handling most of Technical Animations' sales and examined the "pink sheets"—sales records on the stock—with a view toward contacting stockholders and asking them what piece of publicity may have influenced their buying it.

Nearly every stockholder Poser talked to said that a piece in *Time* magazine had motivated them to buy Technical Animations. Checking the broker's entire customer list to learn what the stock's buyers did for a living, Poser, now assisted by several other SEC employees, came across the name of Joseph Purtell, one of the broker's most active traders and *business editor* of *Time* magazine.

Stockbroker records revealed that Purtell would regularly buy several hundred shares of a stock, and then a few days later a very favorable story about the company would appear in the business section of *Time*. Soon after that Purtell would sell his stock, which meantime had risen several points as a result of the *Time* story.

Before the SEC investigation was concluded it was learned that between 1957 and 1961 Purtell had traded in the stocks of twenty-seven corporations which he had favorably reported on in the business section of *Time*.

The practice of promoting stocks on the pages of

investors' newsletters is nothing new—it has been going on for years—but the *Time* case is an indication of what can happen—and could happen again. Purtell had been fired by *Time* for other causes prior to the SEC investigation, but he never paid a fine nor spent a day in jail as a result of his market manipulations.

Back in 1908, by the way, A. N. Ridgeley, publisher of *Ridgeley's Financial Forecasts,* made history when he sued market manipulator James Keene, who failed to keep an agreement to pay Ridgeley for touting the shares of Southern Pacific in his newsletter.

Stock market letters abound today, but research indicates their track record in forecasts is little, if any, better than the behavior of the market as a whole. Six leading investors' newsletters whose forecasts I plotted between 1965 and 1972 fared *worse* than the market.

If I really knew what the market was going to do, I wouldn't sell the information to subscribers for pennies. I'd be in the market to make my fortune.

Unethical business editors and newsletter writers and dishonest corporate managements are not alone in inducing the public to follow the false lights of unsound investment.

SEC Commissioner Sommer reports:

> I have been astonished in the time I have been at the Commission at the evidence of the willingness of auditors to put aside their good judgment and uncritically follow the lead of management. Management asserts that it will get orders several times greater than it has ever achieved and the auditor accepts this as the basis for deferral of massive development costs; management alleges that sales are made with no privilege of return and the auditor accepts such statements while ignoring numerous

> red flags that indicate major changes in selling terms and which suggest that representations are of dubious validity. . . . There are too many cases to write off each as an aberration.
>
> Some managements, with the concurrence of their auditors, are prepared to embellish their performance by the use of accounting tricks which reflect accounting results dramatically different from economic results.

The criticism of accounting "outsiders" like SEC Commissioner Sommer is echoed by accounting "insiders" like Leonard Spacek, senior partner and chairman emeritus of Arthur Andersen & Company, one of America's largest and most respected accounting firms.

This is what Spacek has to say about "generally accepted accounting principles," which are the traditional basis for corporate annual reports and financial data supplied to investors, brokers, and the SEC: "How my profession can tolerate such fiction and look the public in the eye is beyond my understanding. I suppose the answer lies in the fact that if your living depends on playing poker, you can easily develop a poker face. My profession appears to regard a set of financial statements as a roulette wheel to the public investor—and it is his tough luck if he doesn't understand the risks that we inject into the accounting reports."

The stock market is not only the wrong place for individuals, it is increasingly becoming fraught with danger even for investment professionals. During 1974 *The Wall Street Journal* reported that an Oklahoma lawyer, Robert S. Trippet, had pulled off one of the biggest stock market capers in history—an oil-drilling con game that fleeced nearly $100 million from such financial luminaries as Walter Wriston, chairman of the First

National City Bank ($211,000); William H. Morton, president of American Express Company ($57,000); Thomas Gates, former chairman of the Morgan Guaranty Trust Company ($133,000); and the financial writer "Adam Smith" ($110,000).

The case of Trippet's Tulsa-based Home-Stake Production Company isn't out of the courts yet, but whatever happens, the bottom line will probably read ". . . thousands lost millions."

The 1970s swindles of Home-Stake and Equity Funding could have happened any time. Investor losses in those cases can easily be compared to the financial ruin of men and women who lost their savings when the financial mirage of a National Student Marketing or Four Seasons Nursing Homes vanished into thin air. Any of that could have happened in the best of times.

But these are not the best of times. The vast majority of "blue-chip" stocks have fallen to near record lows and some august Wall Street brokerage houses are fleeing the stock market and selling real estate, commodities, and insurance instead. Others are trying their hand at cattle feed-lots, oil drilling, and farming. One firm, First Harlem Securities, is managing a rock combo.

Even such desperate measures are unable to save some firms. Recognize these Wall Street Names—Hayden Stone, Incorporated; Goodbody & Company, Inc.; Blyth & Company, Inc.? Gone, all gone, along with nearly a hundred other liquidated or merged brokers listed in SIPC's 1973 annual report.

Richard H. Jenrette, president of Donaldson, Lufkin & Jenrette, Inc., financial services, predicts the shutdown, merger or buy-out of all but perhaps 110 of the

500 brokerage offices in New York during the next few years.

As of May 1, 1975, fixed brokerage commissions will be a thing of the past and brokers will be competing harder than ever for investors' business. There is talk on Wall Street of selling stocks through department stores, banks, and even at street-corner "stock emporiums," the way New York State promotes off-track betting.

Certainly the vast majority of brokers, corporate managements, lawyers, and accountants are honest; but until the brokerage industry and the SEC remove the welcome mat which is still in place for con men and swindlers, Wall Street remains dangerously mined and booby-trapped for nonprofessionals.

And, as millions of investors now know, common stock is a useless paper shield against the onslaught of real inflation.

In good times, free of government economic mismanagement, common stock *should* be a good investment. Someday the market may be a good place to invest, but not now, not tomorrow—and not the day after.

9

Welcome to the Welfare State

If a private insurance company attempted to sell a plan in Illinois which cost so much and paid so little as Social Security, we would drum them out of the state as frauds.

Illinois Department of Insurance, 1974

What do you call something which takes a bigger bite of your income each year, which forces prices higher and higher, and which touches the wealthy only slightly while materially affecting the lives of middle-income families and the poor?

Call it inflation—and color it Social Security.

During the past twenty years Social Security payroll deductions have grown 800 per cent, more than ten times the cost-of-living increase for the same period. In 1974 Social Security payroll deductions for 50 per cent of the nation's wage earners were greater than the amount they paid in income tax.

Each year, employers are forced to raise prices to keep pace with larger and larger Social Security taxes levied upon them.

Persons over sixty-five years of age who must work to make ends meet are penalized by reduced Social Security benefits, while the executive pension plans, stock options, and money-making business dealings of the more affluent leave their monthly Social Security checks intact.

When the Social Security Administration was established in 1935, payroll deductions of 1 per cent and employer contributions of 1 per cent were expected to fund a plan which would ease the financial burdens of retired workers over sixty-five. Early Social Security checks, first issued in 1940, after the fund had built a reserve, were usually less than $25.00 a month.

Today, maximum benefits to a single retired worker are $3,660 per year. In 1972 Congress pegged benefits to the cost of living and lit the fuse on an inflationary time-bomb that will send both Social Security taxes and benefits out of sight.

By the Social Security Administration's estimate, future annual payments to a single retired worker will soar:

1980	$ 5,580
1990	8,976
2000	15,082
2010	25,693
2020	42,908
2030	71,292

Behind that shiny promise, though, is the fact that price-boosting employer contributions and paycheck-cutting taxes are destined to go up right along with the government's pledge of a free lunch by the swimming pool:

YEAR	EMPLOYER/ EMPLOYEE TAX
1980	$ 825
1990	1,071

YEAR	EMPLOYER/ EMPLOYEE TAX
2000	3,019
2010	4,954
2011 (A major jump is scheduled for this year).	6,005
2020	9,319
2030	15,176

What Congress counted on when it established the cost-of-living escalator was that during the next seventy-five years, wages would rise 5 per cent each year and that the cost of living would rise only 3 per cent annually. That miscalculation is only one of a series of massive errors which have combined to virtually eliminate the fund the government draws on to pay benefits.

The Social Security Administration has grossly miscalculated the rate of inflation; it has ignored changes in the population; and it has time and again increased benefits without raising taxes to compensate.

Even before its recent unfunded cost-of-living giveaway, the Social Security Administration's growing range of benefits read like the list of lifetime prizes offered contestants on a big-time quiz show:

In 1939 widows sixty-five and over of insured workers became eligible to collect benefits, as did dependents.

In 1950 coverage was broadened to include regularly employed farm and domestic workers and was made available on a voluntary basis to state and local government workers and employees of nonprofit organizations.

In 1954 self-employed professionals (with the exception of doctors and lawyers) were added, and ministers were offered voluntary coverage.

In 1956 coverage became available to all self-employed professionals (except doctors) and military personnel and on a voluntary basis to policemen and firemen. Benefits were also extended to permanently disabled workers after age fifty, and the age at which retired female workers became eligible for reduced benefits was lowered to sixty-two.

In 1958 coverage was extended to provide payments to dependents of disabled workers.

In 1960 disabled workers of any age became eligible for benefits and coverage was extended to provide benefits to American citizens employed in the United States by foreign governments.

In 1961 retired male workers, dependent husbands, widowers, and parents of deceased workers became eligible for reduced benefits at age sixty-two.

In 1965 coverage was finally extended to self-employed physicians, and full-time students between ages eighteen and twenty-one became eligible for dependent or survivor benefits. Medicare was enacted, providing hospital insurance for people over sixty-five and, on a voluntary basis, insurance to cover doctor bills.

Coverage was also extended to people over seventy-two who had not worked long enough to qualify for benefits at age sixty-five.

In 1940 when the Social Security Administration issued its first benefit checks, there were 35 million workers and 200,000 beneficiaries, *a ratio of 150 to 1.*

In 1950 there were 48 million workers and 3.5 million beneficiaries, *a ratio of 14 to 1.*

In 1960 there were 72.5 million workers and 14 million beneficiaries, *a ratio of only 5 to 1.*

In 1974 there were 95 million workers and 33 million beneficiaries, *a ratio of about 3 to 1.*

In the year 2000 this ratio will be nearly 2 to 1. By that time, only two workers will be paying taxes for each person receiving benefits!

Though Social Security taxes have climbed 800 per cent during the past twenty years, unfunded benefits have been added and coverage overextended to the point where the so-called Social Security trust fund is on the verge of bankruptcy. Even with planned tax increases, there will soon be nothing left to draw on:

YEAR	FUND SUFFICIENT TO PAY BENEFITS FOR:
1947	17 years, 6 months
1957	3 years, 1 month
1965	1 year, 2 months
1974	8 months
1980 (est.)	0

We don't forecast collapse of the Social Security Administration by 1980. What we do foresee, though, is an 85 per cent probability that very soon the federal government will be forced to embark on a superinflationary borrowing program in an attempt to "bail out" the bankrupt Social Security Administration.

Already the Social Security Administration is using present premiums to pay off present claims. "Operating in this manner," says the head of the Illinois State Insurance Department, "is a fraud because it conceals a state of bankruptcy."

Even if benefits over the next few years are limited to cost-of-living increases, taxpayer hostility toward what is increasingly being called the "Social Security rip-off" precludes the imposition of tax rates which would be high enough to prevent the so-called trust fund from being wiped out.

The cost of Social Security is already so high and its benefits so low compared with private insurance that the Social Security Administration wouldn't have a single taxpayer on its rolls if they were not forced by law to be there.

Social Security offers the cheapest type of life insurance at three to five times the normal rate:

A married twenty-seven-year-old worker with two children and his employer in 1975 must each pay the Social Security Administration $1,400 each year for coverage that would provide $450 per month to the worker's family for twenty years if he died that same year.

Under a private insurance plan, the same worker would pay only $192 a year for coverage that would pay his family $500 a month for the same twenty years.

Social Security provides the least useful type of disability insurance at more than three times the average private insurance company rate:

Social Security disability insurance requires that the total disability be expected to last at least twelve months. And it requires that the beneficiary wait until the beginning of the seventh month before he or she receives any payment at all.

Under many typical private insurance plans costing the same twenty-seven-year-old worker $10 per month, there would be no twelve-month total disability requirement and there would be only a thirty-day waiting period.

The Social Security Administration is guilty of discrimination against "policy holders" that would have its officers in Federal Court if it were a private insurance company:

Retired individuals who benefit from executive retirement plans, who receive stock dividends, and who are in a position to enter money-making ventures which do not constitute "wages" continue to receive the full amount of their Social Security check.

Workers who must hold an additional job to keep their heads above water after they retire have 50¢ deducted from their monthly Social Security check for every dollar above $2,400 which they earn in any year.

Since those who need Social Security the most are usually those who have earned the least, a large majority of workers are calling Social Security's compulsory payroll deductions "rip-off Number One."

There's more good news. During the 1970s, the United States birth rate dropped until there is almost a zero population growth, a development Social Security Administration officials hadn't expected until the twenty-first century.

As a result, when the World War II baby-boom generation is ready to start drawing retirement benefits, there will be very few tax-paying workers around to provide the money.

Still, speak-no-evil officials of the Social Security Administration aren't too concerned. "Look at it this way," says Social Security Administrator James B. Caldwell. "The Social Security Administration could never get so deficient that it will be bankrupt. If you reach that point, the whole system will have collapsed."

"Exactly so," said Alice.

The Mad Hatter opened his eyes very wide on hearing this and turned to the man wearing the blindfold of red tape and asked, "Can you tell me, then, why a raven is like a writing-desk?"

"It is all perfectly clear," the man replied.

"Exactly so," said the Mad Hatter. "Exactly so," replied Alice.

10

The Perpetual Inflation Machine

There is definitely a trend now toward the building of a wage explosion.

Charles A. McDonald,
Office of Wage Stabilization, 1974

For "wage explosion" read "price explosion." In the past wages and prices have been free to rise and fall, acting in balance like stabilizers on an ocean liner, to keep the economy on an even keel.

But during 1973 and 1974, a tidal wave of new union wage contracts pegged to the cost of living threatened to sweep away even the imagined gains of bigger paychecks and more dollars.

Under many of the newly devised agreements of 1974, wages could go up with each rise of the consumer price index, but never down. Since widespread wage increases always lead to widespread price increases, a rise in the cost of living follows each wage increase, setting off yet another round of higher wages and prices.

It was as though an inept "Sorcerer's Apprentice" somewhere in Washington had turned the American economy into a perpetual inflation machine.

In May of 1974 more than 400,000 members of the United Steelworkers Union, plus 36,000 workers in container firms, received cost-of-living pay boosts of 15¢ an hour. Soon afterward the price of steel was increased.

In June 600,000 auto workers in plants operated by General Motors, Chrysler, and Ford received cost-of-living allowances of 13 cents an hour under the "escalator" clause of their contracts with the automobile manufacturers. Soon afterward the big three auto makers announced price increases which, they said, were to compensate for higher labor costs.

Also in June 100,000 members of the United Steelworkers employed at three major aluminum companies received cost-of-living wage adjustments. Both American Can and Alcoa announced that they would seek higher prices to offset increased labor costs.

By the close of 1974 nearly 20 million union workers were covered by cost-of-living labor contracts virtually guaranteeing increases in the prices of a wide spectrum of goods and services. Postal workers received cost-of-living pay increases in November 1973, May 1974, and November 1974. Postal rates, already once raised to accommodate higher labor costs, went up again in early 1976. Postal employees were scheduled to receive at least one cost-of-living pay raise during 1975.

In December 1974 the United Mine Workers capped off a year of attempting to catch up with the runaway cost of living with a contract which provided for a 50 per cent rise in wages and benefits over three years and the UMW's first cost-of-living escalator.

In commenting on the pact, *Time* magazine pointed out:

"The mine settlement is certain to lift the price of

coal—as well as steel, electricity, and myriad consumer products, adding further to oppressive living costs."

The UMW's new work agreement also called for a $900 million increase in royalties which the companies will pay to fund the union's health and retirement programs. Pensioners' monthly retirement checks jumped from $150 to as much as $375.

The United Steelworkers opened another inflationary floodgate in 1974 by negotiating cost-of-living adjustments for members who are already retired.

As other labor contracts came up for renewal, leaders of virtually every major union in the United States were winning cost-of-living wage and retirement benefits as a part of new work agreements.

An October 1974, Bureau of Labor Statistics survey of all labor contracts covering 1,000 or more workers revealed that agreements signed the third quarter of that year included pay increases averaging 11 per cent —double the anti-inflation guideline of 5.5 per cent established by the Nixon administration Pay Board.

No one questions a worker's right to a living wage, nor the right of retired workers to have some kind of protection against the rapid decline of his or her retirement dollar. What must be pointed out is that inflation has already reached the point where it is feeding upon itself.

As this is being written there is no shortage of labor to set employers bidding against each other to fill vacancies on the production line. Unemployment is at its highest rate in years. While American union leaders were obtaining the most costly wage settlements ever won, the President of the United States was making plans for the establishment of the Community Improvement Corps, a $500-million government program to provide jobs for 83,000 unemployed men and women.

A recent survey by Arthur Young & Company, a national accounting firm, confirms that union workers are not alone when it comes to gorging themselves on the empty calories of devalued dollars at the inflationary trough.

Executive salaries advanced 8 per cent during 1973 and the average executive bonus at 300 leading industrial corporations soared 35 per cent. The average executive bonus at the companies surveyed was 44 per cent of the executive's base pay, compared with 36 per cent in 1972 and 28 per cent in 1971.

In what was surely the richest contract ever negotiated by a labor union, the Air Line Pilots Association in September 1974 won 20 per cent pay boosts for Delta Airlines 747-jet captains that put them into the $100,000-a-year income bracket. The agreement also provided pay boosts to other Delta captains and copilots.

Under a new pricing policy that spun the inflationary merry-go-round full circle, the Westinghouse Electric Corporation announced a new pricing policy that would allow the final price of some products to go up as the price of materials and labor goes up. Westinghouse officials said that the new price policy was part of the company's attempt to insulate itself from inflation."

In another example of runaway inflation, the auto insurance industry announced in November 1974 that despite greatly reduced claims, auto insurance rates would be higher in 1975. Although increasing medical costs and higher repair bills were mentioned, insurance company spokesmen said the chief reason car owners' insurance bills will go up is that *the value of insurance com-*

pany stock holdings has been sharply reduced by the sliding stock market. "Higher rates are being sought to offset stock market losses," admitted an official of the industry-owned Insurance Services Office.

There's now little chance that the government or anyone else will be able to turn off the wage-price perpetual inflation machine.

Every economic adviser to the Ford administration has urged against wage or price controls and White House economic counselor Dr. Kenneth Rush admits that, short of controls, there's no way to prevent continued cost-of-living wage hikes which will be passed along to consumers as higher prices.

Although they are experiencing the effect of higher labor costs in most everything they buy, consumers have yet to be hit by the coming round of price increases growing out of cost-of-living pension plan benefits included in the latest turn of the inflationary merry-go-round. Not only are the new plans not funded, but many large companies haven't set aside sufficient money to meet their obligations under previous agreements.

Continental Can is an example. It has a past unfunded pension plan liability of $100 million and now is looking at requirements to come up with an additional $100 million very soon to fund cost-of-living pension adjustments.

According to the March 18, 1974, issue of *Barron's*, "many corporations already are accumulating huge deferred pension plan obligations that are not being reflected realistically on the balance sheets, but sooner or later, will have to be reckoned with."

A recent Greenwich (Connecticut) Research Associates survey of 1,000 of the nation's largest corporations revealed that 21 per cent of the firms surveyed are putting from 25 to 50 per cent of their earnings into pension plans. Nearly 20 per cent of the firms are putting *more* than 50 per cent of earnings into pension plans. "If the trend continues," said the Greenwich report, "these corporations will find themselves in a severe financial squeeze." The costs, bound to increase from year to year as benefits ratchet upward and increasing numbers of workers retire, *must* be paid by the consumer.

There's every indication that cost-of-living pension plans have just begun to spread. United Steelworkers' president I. W. Abel says he expects cost-of-living pension plans soon to be the rule throughout the country. John Tomakyo, head of the steelworkers' pension operations, says the union considers its 65 per cent cost-of-living escalator merely a "foot in the door" and that the union will be trying to improve that coverage when the current three-year contract ends.

The customers of Continental Can, General Motors, IT&T, United States Steel, and nearly every other major American corporation will soon be financing supersocial security programs for most of the 42 per cent of the labor force covered by private pension plans.

The benefits are an illusion since the steelworker who buys a car finances auto workers' retirement, and the auto worker finances the aluminum company retirement plan every time he buys anything made of aluminum.

What hasn't been asked by anyone, apparently, is this question: Who will pay for labor's increased benefits? The answer, of course: the public.

Despite cost-of-living allowances, union workers' wage adjustments only compensate for a portion of the increase in living costs. Real income, for union members and for millions of nonunion workers and self-employed individuals, is slipping. Even in so-called "real dollars" (a term even the government is using more and more often these days), a month's paycheck buys far less than it did a year ago.

If there is a lesson in any of this, it is that inflation is *not* going to be turned around; that too much has *already happened* and is *happening now* for the perpetual inflation machine to be halted before it has converted our currency into meaningless pieces of paper.

11

Food: Who Needs It?

We will see increasing food troubles, not declining food troubles. We will see increasing famine, pestilence, and the extermination of large numbers of people.

Dr. John Knowles, President,
The Rockefeller Foundation, 1974

The soaring price of food, which in 1973 accounted for 51 per cent of America's cost-of-living increase, is diminishing the purchasing power of the dollar faster than any other aspect of inflation.

The cause is classic: too many buyers for a limited supply. The effect: widespread starvation, riots, the toppling of governments, and, very possibly, war. To expect that food prices in the United States will tend to level off any time in the foreseeable future is insanity.

Worldwide demands, coupled with exorbitant petroleum prices, which put fertilizer and fuel for irrigation pumps almost beyond the reach of starving nations and drive up production costs at home, will soon begin to send food prices soaring at exponential rates.

Already 400 million of the world's people exist on near-starvation diets and more than 10,000 starve to death each day. In the cities of India and Bangladesh and Central Africa, the gutters are routinely rid of scores of bodies every morning.

In northern India, trees are stripped of all edible leaves and entire families commit suicide together rather than slowly die one by one. In the Central African nation of Chad, parents recently begged United Nations relief officials not to send medicine during a diphtheria epidemic. It was more merciful, they explained, for their children to die quickly than to slowly waste away from hunger.

During the November 1974 World Food Conference in Rome, former Bangladesh Food Minister Amirul Islam announced that 100,000 people in his country had died in just a few weeks and that 1 million more would die during the coming sixty days unless immediate aid was provided.

In the first nine months of 1973, the sale of pet food in the United States increased 12 per cent compared to an estimated zero increase in the pet population, and the head of the Center for Science in the Public Interest estimated that by mid-1974, one third of the pet food sold in ghetto areas was being consumed by people.

Arrests for food theft from supermarkets during 1974 soared nearly 800 per cent above similar arrests during 1973, although store owners were reluctant to prosecute in obvious hardship cases.

World demands upon the United States food supply cannot be met. CARE cut 10 million children from its relief rolls, and Catholic Relief services today feed six million fewer people than a short time ago. America's "Food for Peace" program is shrinking from both lack of food and money.

Soaring populations in underfed countries are forcing

foreign governments to bid against the American people for food produced in the United States.

Russia's well-publicized 400-million-bushel purchase of one fourth of America's 1972 wheat crop served to distract attention from the vast quantities of United States food which other foreigners buy in competition with American families.

In 1975 the food budgets of American families began another upward spiral when the United States agreed to sell the Soviet Union a *minimum* of six million tons of wheat and corn annually for five years. Pennsylvania State University economist George Brandow estimates that, at the very least, the agreement will raise U.S. retail food prices 2.4 per cent per year during the life of the agreement.

Although a provision in the accord states that the U.S.S.R. *may* sell the U.S. 64 million barrels of oil annually during the agreement's five-year time period, there is no requirement that the U.S.S.R. provide the petroleum, nor is there any requirement that the oil be sold at prices below, or even equal to, OPEC prices.

In 1973 Communist China became the biggest importer of U.S. wheat, quietly purchasing more than 100 million bushels from American grain dealers at the same bargain-basement prices the Russians got. That same year Japan bought 64 million bushels, India bought 51 million, South Korea bought 38 million, and Brazil bought 33 million bushels.

Recent *increases* in Japanese food purchases surpass all of Russia's purchases for 1973.

Two thirds of American wheat, more than half of our soybeans, and over 20 per cent of our corn is exported. During 1974 food departing the United States fed one fourth of the world's population!

The price of American grain has been bid up by foreign buyers and bid up again by Americans competing for what wheat remains. Wheat which sold for $1.35 a bushel in 1972, for $1.85 in 1973, and for $3.40 at the close of 1974 was expected to be costing American buyers $5.00 per bushel by the end of 1976.

Higher prices for grain mean higher feed costs for cattle producers, raising the price of meat. The same costly feed raises the expense of feeding dairy cows, boosting the cost of milk. Farmers, tempted by these demands for grain, plant wheat and corn instead of green vegetables—so vegetable shortages develop. Expensive chicken feed makes poultry cost more.

Food prices will surely continue to soar and there is an 80 per cent probability that food costs and shortages will produce "runaway" food price increases during the next few years for the following reasons, among others:

World population continues to rise at the rate of 1.4 million every week.

Petroleum costs will continue to increase.

Fertilizer costs are increasing.

The costs of bringing additional land under cultivation are so high that the effect of any increased food in the marketplace is more than offset by the expense of preparing and cultivating the land.

According to the November 14, 1974, *Wall Street Journal:*

> Inflation, energy, population, and food problems are so interwoven that the mess is enormous. Inflation has soared to the point where the poor nations of the world are being priced out of food markets. The quadrupling of petroleum prices in the last two years has led to fertilizer shortages, to a dearth of fuel for irrigation pumps, and to trans-

portation difficulties. The exploding world population adds 1.4 million additional food consumers each week to the world's total. And food production is leveling off.

How serious, and how long-term, are the price pressures pushing up the cost of food?

World population. One way of putting the world population explosion in perspective is to realize that it's been coming for a long time:

In 1650 the world population was about half a billion and grew at the rate of 0.3 per cent a year, meaning a doubling time of 250 years.

In 1970 the world population totaled 3.6 billion and was increasing at 2.1 per cent a year, meaning a doubling time of 33 years.

Unless there is a sharp rise in the death rate, by the year 2000 we can expect a world population of seven billion.

Unfortunately, the highest birth rates are in countries which are already unable to feed themselves and which, generally, have the strongest religious and social bias against birth control:

AREA	ANNUAL GROWTH RATE
Brazil	3.0%
Southeast Asia	2.6%
Nigeria	2.4%
India	2.5%
China	1.7%

India's annual growth rate will double its current population of nearly 600 million by the year 2000 and the numbers of food consumers in many other starving countries will double before or shortly after then.

There's little inclination to reduce birth rates in countries that need food the most, and tacit approval to continue high birth rates was given by the Vatican during the 1974 World Food Conference in Rome. Accusing the rich nations of the world of trying to "impose birth control on the poor to keep them poor," Pope Paul VI declared that "it is inadmissible that those who have control of the wealth and resources of mankind should try to solve the problem of hunger by forbidding the poor to be born."

The Communist Chinese government argues for continued high birth rates in developing countries, claiming that "the large population of the Third World is an important condition for the fight against imperialism."

Even doubling food production overnight would do little more than delay the return of mass starvation for a short time unless world population growth is more or less stabilized.

In raw numbers, then, world population is growing at the rate of 200,000 additional mouths to feed every day —far faster than our ability to produce food. Nearly 460 million exist on near-starvation diets now and at least 15 million are expected to die from lack of food during 1975.

High Petroleum Costs. The recent 400 per cent increase in the price of petroleum by the Organization of Petroleum Exporting Countries (OPEC) put the purchase of fertilizers and pesticides made with petroleum products beyond the reach of many underdeveloped nations and stilled irrigation pumps which mean the difference between life and death to crops—and those who tend them—in many parts of the world. Abundant fertilizer would go a long way toward intensifying the yield of land already under cultivation, but increased fertilizer costs threaten to sweep underdeveloped nations with a plague of starvation.

Nitrogen fertilizers and anhydrous ammonia are derived from natural gas and have in many countries become prohibitively expensive. India's bill for purchasing the fertilizer she needs in addition to that she manufactures would cost $300 million—more than the entire amount of her foreign exchange. The Indian government says it can only afford to buy half of the fertilizer it needs.

"For every dollar of fertilizer Bangladesh cannot buy this year," warns a UN relief agency official, "it will have to import $5 in food next year. There is no assurance that she will be able to buy enough food, even at twice today's prices."

Since fertilizer plants also require great amounts of energy, many located in underdeveloped countries are running at less than capacity because of high petroleum costs. India's fertilizer plants, for example, are running only at 50 per cent of capacity.

High petroleum costs are cutting the world's food supply in other ways. Across the parched fields of India and Bangladesh, Africa and Latin America, irrigation pumps stand idle because farmers and the governments of underdeveloped nations don't have the money to buy petroleum which costs five times more than it did a few years ago.

Also dangerously reduced is the amount of pesticides which farmers in underdeveloped nations have available to protect crops from even normal insect populations. With crop yields already reduced by lack of fertilizer and marginal crop-areas returned to pasture land due to lack of irrigation, any outbreak of insect damage could easily destroy a helpless nation's food supply.

Farm product costs in the United States are also

highly affected by the cost of fuel. While American farm production doubled, farm fuel consumption increased 400 per cent. Because less fertile land is being pressed into production, farmers get only half as much food per gallon as they used to.

Even before fuel price increases forced starving nations to reduce food production, total world food yields were barely keeping half a step ahead of soaring population growth in the Near and Far East, Africa, and Latin America. Now that crop yields are edging downward, foreign demands for U.S. food grains are mounting.

Today, food production uses 12 per cent of the world's total energy. If we attempt to provide even 1974's bare subsistence diet to the 4 billion world population forecast by the end of 1975, it would require 1,500 billion gallons of fuel annually and would consume all known petroleum resources by 1984.

Limited Farmland. Recent United Nations figures indicate that there are about 8 billion acres of land in the world suitable for cultivation. More than half of this land—the most productive, the most accessible—is already under cultivation. The other half will require extraordinary amounts of money and manpower for people to reach, clear, fertilize, irrigate and cultivate before food can be produced there in any significant quantity.

According to a 1970 UN Food and Agricultural Organization report:

> In Southeast Asia, in some countries of Eastern Asia, in the Near East and North Africa, and in certain areas of Latin America and Africa, there is almost no hope of expanding the arable area. In most of Latin America and Africa south of the Sahara there are possibilities for expanding culti-

vated areas, but the costs for development are high and it will often be more economical to intensify utilization of areas already settled.

According to the United States Department of Agriculture, there are 264 million acres in the United States that could be cultivated but are now being used as pasture and timberland and would be too costly to convert to farming. Much other uncultivated land is so poor—and so inaccessible—that the expense of farming it would be prohibitive.

There is one way that much of our nation's productive farmland can be retained in production: stop urbanization. Each year more than 600,000 acres of fertile land is paved over with highways, housing developments, and shopping centers.

But many state taxes based upon the *potential* or *possible* use of a piece of land, rather than its *actual* use, will have to be changed if farmers are not to be forced to sell out. When their near-suburban property is taxed at high urban rates because it "could" be used as a shopping center or housing development, many farmers must stop producing food. Every time a farmer is squeezed out of business, prices you pay at the supermarket edge a little higher.

Weather. At the close of 1974, world grain reserves were sufficient only for twenty-two days and were forecast to fall to only an eight-day supply by late spring, 1975, making weather and climatic changes a major concern.

United States' crops of both corn and soybeans were far short of expectations during 1974 because of excessive spring rains, a summer drought, and an early frost. While great floods devastated the Bangladesh harvest, the first drought in years ruined the rice crop of western India.

With food reserves in 1975 at their lowest level since the end of World War II, the consequences of a severe drought and the coming cooler climate cycle can be expected to turn the demand for food into violence.

"If a severe drought [in the U.S.] occurs, as I think it may," says former Department of Agriculture economist Lester Brown, "we will see consumer and civil unrest which could easily topple ten or fifteen governments."

Economist Robert Heilbroner fears that, "even hungry, poor states might soon get the nuclear arms with which to terrorize wealthy Western countries."

While no one expects evidence of a coming ice age to appear on the northern horizon in the immediate future, it's now clear that the world is moving into a cooling cycle which is trimming weeks from the growing season in the earth's "breadbasket" middle latitudes.

The last chilly phase of what climatologists believe is a 200-year cycle brought agricultural disaster to much of Europe. Many of today's hybrid crops, developed during the recent warming cycle, are particularly vulnerable to damage by cold.

The possibility of climatic disasters is the special concern of Frank McKnight of the Agriculture Department's Commodity Credit Corporation. "Of course we're concerned," he says, "and we're making studies, but beyond that, there's not much we can do. We might all pray for good weather—yes, maybe that's what we ought to be doing."

Lack of Water. The soaring world population will increase the demand for water 240 per cent by the year 2000. All of the relatively inexpensive dam projects have been completed and the cost of new, extremely expensive dams puts them beyond the grasp of the countries that need them the most. The only option left is to use available water more efficiently.

New Kinds of Food. New breeds of grain are being developed which provide more protein and which might be able to grow on poor land and under adverse weather conditions, but their development takes more time than the underfed and starving can afford.

At Purdue University in 1973 researchers bred a new variety of high-protein sorghum, but only after seven years of work analyzing more than 10,000 varieties of grain. And the scientists say that "it could be another ten years before the grain will be ready for planting on a significant scale."

Even the most glittering answers sometimes fall far short of their promise. Special hybrids of the much-publicized "green revolution" were and are highly dependent upon irrigation and fertilizer and are extremely susceptible to vagaries in the weather. High fuel and fertilizer costs are now turning the fields of the green revolution into a withered wasteland.

Miracle pesticides, which at first seemed to offer hope, now appear to have allowed the survival of the "unfittest" of crops while breeding hordes of pesticide-resistant insects.

American ranchers are importing leaner breeds of European cattle which are ready for market in half the time required for fatter stock traditionally consumed in the United States. But with cattle providing far less protein than is available from the grain used to feed it, shelves of soybean-based meat substitutes such as texturized vegetable protein (TVP) may soon replace the meat freezers in American and European food markets.

The Japanese are exploring the possibilities of catching krill, shrimplike shellfish high in protein. Though they're relatively plentiful and fairly easy to catch, the Japanese are finding they have to travel as far as the Antarctic for a sizable catch. And there are other problems.

"Technically we can catch krill without too much difficulty," says Japanese biochemist Dr. Minoru Okada, "but processing it on the boat is extremely difficult to set up. The krill will only keep for about two hours after being taken from the cold water so we have to process and store it aboard the vessel."

The Antarctic krill-catching season is short, so the expensive factory ships could only be used for a short time each year. Costs are also high because the ships must travel so far.

Generally, efforts at "farming the sea" have been disappointing. Costs have been too high and experts say there's no reason to expect the sea to provide substantially more food in the years ahead. Statistics show declining catches during the past few years due to pollution and overfishing.

Long-term food production efforts, plus reduced birth rates and new eating habits, will eventually ease food shortages and allow some drop in the cost of food. But the key word is "eventually" and until "eventually" becomes "here and now," there is no chance that food prices will decline; there is every certainty that they will climb at increasing rates.

Short of buying and storing vast quantities of food for future use in times of inflation and shortage, an American consumer's best long-term protection against runaway food prices is to invest in a commodity—

Which will increase in "price" during inflation.

Which is easy to store and move.

Which you can readily exchange for food.

The "real money" of gold and silver meets these requirements very well.

12

Yours: The New Fireproof Mortgage

> *Given a twenty-five-year, $30,000 mortgage in its third year of repayment, an interest rate increase from 6 to 8¼ per cent under the proposed variable rate mortgage plan would mean that the mortgage would become indefinite. It could* never *be repaid at the original $193 monthly payment rate.*
>
> Professor George Kaufman,
> University of Oregon, 1974

The Federal Home Loan Bank Board (FHLBB), the agency which regulates savings and loan associations, is trying to launch the banker-sponsored *variable rate mortgage,* in which mortgage interest rates and/or monthly payments are free to fluctuate up or down with general interest rates.

FHLBB chairman Thomas Bomar, with more than a little help from powerful mortgage bankers, is quietly lobbying in Congress for passage of legislation which would transfer the burden of climbing home loan interest rates from bankers to borrowers.

Under the variable rate mortgage proposal, changes in mortgage interest rates would be pegged into an index which relates both to mortgage market and money market interest rates.

Increases could be imposed no more often than every six months, with a maximum ½ per cent rise at any one time. The maximum upward adjustment would be limited to 2½ per cent.

Complete disclosure, including the potential maximum cost, would have to be made before initiating the agreement.

Mortgage bankers claim that the nationwide adoption of variable rate mortgages would make sufficient money available to turn on home-building and make money available once again for Americans to buy their dream houses.

The way Bomar sees it, the fixed rate loan forces lenders to guess what inflation rates will be in the future and then set a rate high enough so that they will have a "real" return after the reduced value of repayment dollars is taken into account. The result, claims Bomar, is that

> . . . the effects of inflation are not borne by all citizens but are disproportionately loaded on those few seeking a loan. For every homeowner sitting snugly with a 5 or 6 per cent loan, there is a disappointed young family out there shut out of the home market because of 10 per cent interest rates and huge down-payment requirements.

We suspect that Bomar's concern is more for the welfare of mortgage bankers than for young families who would supposedly be besieged with home-loan offers if only Congress could be persuaded to transfer responsibility of handicapping future inflation rates from the computer-equipped offices of bankers to the kitchen tables of borrowers.

Advance Mortgage Corporation executive vice-president Robert J. Mylod has proposed three mortgage plans designed to protect bankers from rampant inflation:

1. The mortgage interest could be adjusted once every year according to an inflation index and the interest portion of the monthly payment adjusted accordingly. [This means that in some years borrowers might make no headway at all in paying off mortgages and could find themselves saddled with higher interest rates *and* higher monthly payments.]

2. The mortgage could be written for five or ten years but payments would be keyed to a longer term. Then, at the end of the mortgage period, the remaining balance would be renewed at the then-current interest rate. [This plan provides no guarantee that the lender *will* renew the mortgage nor does it guarantee that if interest rates have dropped a new mortgage *would* be rewritten at the lower rate.]

3. The amount of inflation as measured by the consumer price index would be added to the principal balance annually. [On a new mortgage with an unpaid principal of $30,000, a 10 per cent annual inflation rate would add $3,000 to the principal at the end of twelve months—an amount equal to twelve payments of $250. Given a 10 per cent inflation rate, this arrangement would leave the borrower owing the bank *more money* at the end of the year than when he signed his mortgage.]

The Advance Mortgage Corporation's proposal would provide mortgage bankers with even better cost-of-living protection than the most hard-won union work agreements. The mortgage bankers' plan provides 100 per cent inflation protection, while new union contracts provide wage adjustments which cover only a part of the cost-of-living increase.

Apparently mortgage bankers are convinced that interest rates will continue their upward climb for quite a while—long enough, certainly, to affect the amount of their profit on a thirty-year mortgage.

The University of Oregon's Professor George Kaufman points out what even a small rise in mortgage interest rates does to the ultimate cost of a house. Given the same $30,000, twenty-five-year mortgage used in his example cited at the beginning of this chapter, Dr. Kaufman says:

> If the interest was raised from 6 to 8 per cent—a modest enough figure in these times—the monthly payment would increase from $193 to $228. Stretching out the payments has its problems, too. In the same case, the payment period would grow from twenty-two years to forty-five years and cost the homeowner $53,000 in *additional interest.*

AFL-CIO President George Meany notified the House Banking Committee, which would consider any variable interest rate legislation, that the labor federation strongly opposed the Federal Home Loan Bank Board's variable interest rate proposal.

Meany, along with United Auto Workers president Leonard Woodcock, feels that variable interest rates are inflationary and would force labor to press for additional cost-of-living wage increases. William Taylor, director of the Center for National Policy Review, urges that action on variable interest rate mortgages be delayed. Taylor, presumably speaking for the Center, says that the time has come "for a fundamental restructuring of the nation's financial institutions."

One thing that mortgage bankers aren't talking about is the fact that rampant inflation has already devalued the buying power of paper dollars to the extent that few people can acquire enough of them to buy a house.

Since January 1972 the price of an average new house in the United States has soared from $24,700 to $37,100. Homes in many urban areas are much higher. A house costing $31,700 in Detroit in October of 1974 would cost $41,100 in Denver, $51,300 in Boston, and $56,000 in Houston.

Says Louis Chairman, executive vice-president of the Builders' Association of Greater Boston, "Your average guy who's making $20,000 a year; well, he's pretty much out of the ballpark by now. The homes cost too much and the down payments are just too high."

Chicago's large First Federal Savings & Loan Association now makes home loans only to regular customers from whom it demands 50 per cent down on a twenty-five-year mortgage which has an annual effective interest rate of 11¼ per cent.

By late 1974 the declining value of the dollar brought on the most severe housing downturn on record. Federal Reserve officials expressed concern about the collapse of the homebuilding industry as they watched homebuilder bankruptcies soar to more than 900 from January through July 1974. Scores of the bankrupt builders were large national concerns.

According to the National Association of Home Builders, the industry has a 10.6 per cent unemployment rate, double the national rate. "The country," says Atlanta homebuilder Charles Sheron, "is in a recession; the housing industry is in a depression."

Housing has become a focal point of the current rampant inflation in the United States as soaring costs of labor, land, materials, maintenance, and interest rates price home ownership out of the reach of more than two thirds of American families.

Many families are turning to what is clearly a second-choice home ownership option: the condominium. But many families see condominium life as too crowded, too noisy, and too regimented. Still, condominium building permits are up 50 per cent compared to single family homes, and clusters of condominium halfway houses are increasingly shouldering their way into neighborhoods formerly the preserve of single-family units.

Families have little choice but to say good-by to yet another supposedly secure part of the American Dream as the declining dollar pulls the rug out from under cherished plans to someday own their own home.

Washington, D.C., builder-architect Sam Dunn, who's given up on home construction and turned to remodeling, says he sees inflation everywhere he looks:

Bricks which cost him $69 a thousand in 1973 cost him $93 in 1974—a 35 per cent increase.

Mortar, $1.80 a bag in 1973, cost $2.10 by mid-1974—a 17 per cent increase.

Nails, 30¢ a pound in 1973, jumped to 36¢ a pound in 1974—up 20 per cent.

Vinyl asbestos tile (a part-petroleum product), $10.40 a box in 1973, skyrocketed to $16.40 in 1974—an increase of 58 per cent.

Roofing asphalt (another petroleum product), $4.35 per five-gallon pail in 1973, cost $6.50 in mid-1974—a jump of 49 per cent.

Copper tubing, 84¢ a foot in 1973, rose to $1.18 a foot in less than twelve months.

Many small builders who don't have the funds or

credit to buy all the materials for a job when they sign the contract are unable to give potential buyers a firm bid and are being driven out of business, leaving the field open for large builders who are free to raise prices further, unhampered by normal competition.

All of the price increases in building materials may not be "real." Suppliers of steel reinforcing bars in several areas of the United States had been telling builders that the standard-size bars were unavailable. To get any bars at all, builders were forced to purchase them several sizes longer than needed, thus forcing up housing costs and allowing the building materials suppliers to sell bars with a higher profit margin.

In August 1974 one Florida grand jury handed down indictments against four major wholesale construction materials companies who were allegedly practicing price gouging in that state.

The Ford administration says it would like to help the thousands of American families who no longer can afford even the gasoline for a Sunday drive to look at dream houses. But the deflated currency of today's inflation was printed yesterday, and any political remedy can only further debase the paper dollar.

In October 1974 the President signed into law the Brooke-Cranston Bill, which will pump $7.75 billion in (inflationary) federal funds into the residential mortgage market during the following twelve months. The money is sufficient to finance more than 250,000 new houses, but nothing short of additional printing-press money can put significant numbers of homebuilders back to work until after the nation suffers a corrective depression which will enable the economy to return to an economic base of "real money."

13

Money
The Advancing ~~Energy~~ Crisis

The wisest and most conservative men in the economic and financial communities have begun to talk helplessly about the threat of an onrushing, worldwide financial calamity in many respects as serious as the great depression of the 1930s. The "energy crisis" is mis-called; it is a money crisis rather than an energy crisis.

Joseph Alsop, Columnist, 1974

Political analyst Joseph Alsop is right. There is practically as much oil, and just as much coal, and just as much natural gas today as there was before the Organization of Petroleum Exporting Countries (OPEC) raised prices 400 per cent. Oil is just as easy to pump today as it was yesterday. The difference is that *the price is higher.*

Energy consumption is increasing—and of course no mineral resource can last forever—but the current "energy crisis" has been brought on by the *price* of oil, not a shortage of it.

Beyond being responsible for thousands of starvation deaths in underfed nations, the high price of oil—up to $11 a barrel by the end of 1974—is tipping the world economic scales toward runaway inflation. I foresee that American currency will lose an additional annual 15 to 25 per cent of its purchasing power during 1975–76 because of:

soaring worldwide demand for U.S. food, which will bid up prices at home;

additional petroleum-related food production cost increases due to high fertilizer, insecticide, animal feed, power, and fuel costs;

continuing upward adjustment of a wide range of prices to compensate for high-priced petroleum-based products such as plastics, petrochemicals, building materials, etc.;

continuing increases in the price of manufactured goods which require huge amounts of energy to produce, such as electricity and steel;

worsening of the United States balance of payments.

Economists now admit that high-priced oil is responsible for at least 25 per cent of the U.S. inflation rate, rather than 2 per cent as originally estimated. But the full effect of "precious" oil has yet to work its way through the American economy.

Wholesale price increases usually take six months or so to work their way through to the consumer. Basic material price increases often take a year finding their way into the retail market. "Raw" material price increases—such as the price of ore or more expensive water for farmers or oil, where oil is a "raw" material such as in petrochemical production—take even longer to make their mark at the cash register.

In April 1975, after the first shock wave of the fuel crisis had passed through the Americn economy and consciousness, the U. S. Water Resources Council, under the direction of Interior Secretary Rogers C. B. Morton, announced that the energy shortage may soon trigger an even worse water crisis.

Energy figured heavily in the Water Resources Council's conference because virtually every proposed method of increasing energy production places extraordinary demands on water supplies.

"Today our water requirements are snowballing," stated the Water Resources Council's final report, "As we evaluate requirements for 1985, we can already see that a water crisis is in the making.

"If we were to stop the development of additional water resources now, by the year 2000 there would be few areas of the nation with an ample water supply at all times and many areas with a chronically short supply."

The effect of costly water upon food and manufacturing costs can not be overlooked.

The intense demand-push competition for the by-products of oil is multiplying the inflationary effect of its $11-a-barrel price far more than first realized.

The United States balance-of-payments deficit (the last item on the list above) is solely related to oil. In 1973 the United States earned a $1.3-billion trade surplus, but 1974's trade deficit was $5 billion. From January through August of 1974, for example, U.S. oil imports ran $11.4 billion *more* than during the same period of 1973. If oil prices had merely been raised 200 per cent, the United States would still have managed to earn a balance-of-payments surplus for 1974.

The *Christian Science Monitor* estimates that without a sharp reduction in foreign oil imports, "the [yearly] balance-of-payments deficit is likely to run between $6 and $12 billion for the foreseeable future."

By the end of last year, the oil-importing countries of the world owed the producing countries no less than $50 billion. International economists predict that by the end of 1975 the world's oil-buying nations will owe the oil producers an *additional* $50 billion and that the debt will continue to climb.

By the end of 1974 the oil-producing nations will have earned more than $100 billion in foreign exchange. By 1980 they could pile up gold, silver, and foreign exchange which would give them reserves of more than $650 billion. By comparison, United States gold reserves were $15 billion as of December 31, 1974.

In very little time, the staggering sums paid to OPEC nations threaten to bring about collapse of the monetary system on which our currency is based. Knowing this, the OPEC nations will now accept payment only in currencies which are convertible to gold, and they are acquiring gold bullion at rates which are tempered solely by the knowledge that more rapid purchases would only drive up the price.

One of those concerned about the river of funds flowing into the Near East is Chase Manhattan Bank chairman David Rockefeller, who feels that the "existing financial system may not be able to stand the strain of the sudden transfer of tens of billions of dollars a year from the oil-importing to the oil-exporting nations."

As the transfer of wealth to the Near East continues, fear of economic instability and political crisis grows. At a joint meeting of the World Bank and International Monetary Fund in Washington, D.C., in the fall of

1974, delegates from more than a hundred nations heard predictions that one or more oil-starved nations might soon be forced to resort to military intervention in the Persian Gulf to secure petroleum resources.

Almost every delegate agreed that unreasonably high oil prices were accelerating inflation, provoking recession, causing unemployment, and threatening collapse of international monetary systems. At the meeting, United States Secretary of State Henry Kissinger expressed grave concern about the effect of high-cost oil upon the economy of Europe.

From its headquarters in London, the International Institute for Strategic Studies announced that it regards the use of oil as a weapon by the OPEC nations as "the greatest immediate threat to world economic and political stability. The rich industrial countries are threatened," warns the Institute, "and so are the oil-poor developing nations such as India, Bangladesh and Pakistan."

Quietly the OPEC nations have been investing huge sums in American corporations, in many cases buying control. Like anyone else making overseas investments, the oil producers will want to see a reasonable return, now considered to be about 10 per cent. These profits will flow out of the American economy, debilitating it even more than if they were dollars taken out of circulation by the Federal Reserve. At a time when the economy is already depressed, that kind of financial drain is another armful of straws on the back of a faltering American currency.

The oil producers aren't talking about the extent of their American investments, but there are figures available on what amounts to only the first day of their worldwide corporate shopping spree. By the end of

1975 the value of oil-producing nations' overseas holdings is expected to be $100 billion—$10 billion *more* than the value of *all* U.S. overseas investments since 1900.

OPEC leaders, who view the depressed state of the American stock market as a chance to buy out the bargain basement, show no inclination to temper their purchases. "Americans," asserts the Shah of Iran, "buy majority interests in European companies and this astonishes nobody. But when we buy as little as 25 per cent, so-called liberals profess to be shocked."

The obstreperous OPEC nations will be in the petroleum market driver's seat for some time to come. Compared to 1974, proven U.S. reserves of 45 billion barrels (including Alaska), the OPEC's 1974 resources are formidable, for example: Iraq, 32 billion barrels; Iran, 60 billion; Kuwait, 64 billion; Libya, 26 billion; and Saudi Arabia, 132 billion. Venezuela, Latin America's largest current oil producer, is estimated to have no more than 15 billion barrels in proven reserves.

For a time, after the discovery of major oil deposits in Alaska, that state's frozen North Slope was considered the great white hope of the oil-hungry "Lower Forty-eight." Geologists are sure the 200-square-mile oil field near Prudhoe Bay holds at least 10 billion barrels.

The first pipeline to move Alaskan oil out—at the rate of perhaps 1.3 billion barrels a day—will be completed in 1977. From the port of Valdez, 800 miles south of Prudhoe, tankers will carry the oil the remainder of the way to refineries in the Lower Forty-eight.

That's the good news.

The bad news is that the expense of getting and moving Alaskan oil is so high that some oilmen predict it may cost as much as the OPEC's $11-a-barrel by the time it leaves the North Slope.

Oil companies paid $900 million just for leases at Prudhoe Bay. Minimum estimates for the trans-Alaska pipeline from Prudhoe to Valdez run to $5 billion. None of this counts the cost of exploration or production.

Canada's oil potential lies to the southeast of Prudhoe in 19,000 square miles of tar sands in northern Alberta. About 55,000 barrels a day were moving out of northern Alberta during early 1975, and four Canadian and American oil companies sharing the $1.3-billion project hope to be producing 125,000 barrels a day by 1977. Once in full swing, the project may be extracting 500,000 barrels a day. But its cost is high, and little of this oil is expected to reach the United States.

More than a ton of dirt must be moved and two tons of tar sand processed to obtain each barrel of oil. Canadian officials figure the total investment involved in getting the oil out will be ten times greater than the entire cost of the St. Lawrence Seaway, and that was $470 million!

Canada's arctic natural gas will be expensive. By latest Canadian Energy Office estimates, the gas will cost, sometime in 1979, slightly more than double current prices.

Not that Canada expects to be selling the United States much of her natural gas or oil. Canada currently sends about 1 billion barrels of oil a day into the United States, but will soon begin cutting back on such exports because of Canada's own needs. Canada's Energy Minister Donald MacDonald states that "Canada has no intention of becoming party to an energy-sharing policy to which Canada contributes her resources and the United States contributes its shortages."

Part of Mexico's recent estimated 19-billion-barrel oil discovery should be available to the United States, but only for a price. During his October 1974 meeting with President Ford, Mexican President Luis Echeverría Álvarez said his country's new oil fields will be "exploited in a profoundly nationalistic" manner.

So while Alaskan oil will gradually become available in the Lower Forty-eight beginning in 1977, its cost is likely to be as great as OPEC oil. Canada's oil won't be available at any price, and Mexico's will be available only in limited amounts—and it too will be expensive.

United States oil? The Federal Energy Administration reports, at best, only a fifteen-year supply of oil left in the United States including Alaska, known offshore resources, and the costly-to-extract shale oil.

Attaining the potential of other energy sources such as atomic power, synthetic oils, solar and thermal energy, and the use of tides and wind and magnetohydrodynamics to generate electricity are all relatively far distant and some are extremely expensive.

All of the exotic alternatives fall far short of oil as "complete" energy sources. Atomic power might replace oil's electricity-producing function, but it isn't a source of fertilizer, asphalt roofing, or petrochemicals. Synthetic oils can perform some of the natural oil's lubricating functions, but they are far too expensive to use as diesel fuel or heating oil.

In attempting to develop a response to the oil-money crisis, the United States is faced with two alternatives: coal and conservation. Neither is very promising.

A study by the Federal Energy Administration (FEA) published in late 1974 reveals that when the six-month Arab oil embargo lowered U.S. oil consumption 14 per cent, it cost 500,000 jobs and reduced the gross national product by $15 billion.

With many thousands more unemployed now than during the embargo and with the gross national product far below its oil embargo level, the federal government will have to perform extraordinary economic surgery to materially cut oil consumption and stem the balance-of-payments hemorrhage without killing the patient.

The government's handbook for performing its oil-import surgery is the Federal Emergency Administration's *Project Independence Blueprint,* a 980-page volume prepared by a team of 750 experts and analysts using a computer model to determine the effects of a wide spectrum of import-cutting actions upon the economy.

Project Independence Blueprint suggests that an accelerated supply policy of full-speed, "damn-the-torpedoes" development of Alaskan oil fields and off-shore drilling, plus relaxation of environmental laws, could reduce oil imports from 5 to 1.5 million barrels a day by 1985.

A second *Blueprint* option would reduce the growth of oil consumption by continuing the 55-miles-per-hour speed limit, by developing energy-saving appliances and lighting standards, by encouraging the use of mass transit, and by a mandatory requirement that autos deliver at least 20 miles per gallon of gasoline. By 1985, states the report, these measures could reduce oil imports from 10 million barrels a day to about 8.2 million barrels a day.

A separate option presented by *Blueprint* is the stockpiling of enough oil to carry the United States through a year-long, 1-million-barrel-a-day embargo. The program would cost $15 billion, but could save as much as $99 billion in the event of an embargo, states the report.

The Ford Foundation, in a 511-page study, *A Time to Choose,* recommends its own version of surgery and a low-calorie diet to alleviate America's money-energy crisis:

Elimination of utility-rate sliding scales which provide lower unit power costs to large consumers. Higher rates would also be charged to peak-period power guzzlers.

Purchase tax on large, low-gas-mileage cars and tax credits for owners of efficient cars.

Tougher insulation standards for Federal Housing Administration (FHA) homes, plus easy credit for improved home insulation.

Establish auto gas-mileage goal of 33 mpg.

According to the Ford Foundation's experts, their program could reduce the growth of U.S. energy use from 4.5 per cent a year to 2 per cent a year by 1985.

Not surprisingly, the FEA's *Project Independence Blueprint,* which offers a series of hard-driving development options, is favored by the oil industry and auto makers over the Ford Foundation's more conservation- and environment-oriented *A Time to Choose.* In both instances, though, the thing to keep your eye on is the date they both talk about as the time when the patient should be able to leave the hospital: 1985.

In the meantime, America is going to be using a lot more coal. The supply is plentiful; the FEA estimates there's enough easy-to-mine coal to meet U.S. needs for 200 years. But the nation is generally unprepared to make use of it.

It will take at least three years to provide the equipment for the 50 per cent of America's utilities which now use oil to convert to coal for power production. The target date for converting oil-fired power plants to coal is 1980.

Most coal will be used in the Northeast, but much pollution-free coal is located in Montana, Colorado, Wyoming, North Dakota, and Utah. Railroads are unequipped to handle it and can't be ready to do so for several years.

Western coal has relatively high concentrates of uranium, a potentially ominous unknown that has the FEA worried about the possible harmful effects of burning it.

Comparing the cost of coal use to oil use is complicated by the fact that neither is a direct substitute for the other. Oil's by-products are costly to obtain from other sources and coal's polluting qualities and transportation costs add more to the expense of using it than the $15-a-ton average price would suggest.

In the absence of tough federal strip-mining controls, much of the coal-rich West could become a wasteland by the time coal producers are through with it. Then, too, coal mining is dangerous. The injury rate of coal miners is ten times as great as the injury rate of auto workers.

And coal presents its own set of inflationary pressures. The 1974 price of coal was up 61 per cent over 1973 and is expected to nearly double its 1973 price by the end of 1975.

Whatever happens with coal, the money-energy crisis will not be easing for at least five years, if even then. United States proposals for an organization of petroleum-importing countries are founded on the premise that reduced consumption by importing nations would start a corner-filling-station-type oil price-war among the petroleum producers.

The treasuries of the OPEC countries are already so filled that they could close down and go fishing until the oil-importing countries came begging. Any reduction in imports by the United States and other major consumers will probably be met by balancing production cut-backs by the OPEC nations.

Any changes in the price of imported oil will be up, not down. Remoteness and the amount of inflation which has already taken place make it likely that the price of newly produced U.S. oil will be at least equal to OPEC prices by the time it begins to flow.

The OPEC nations have both challenged United States economic leadership *and* chosen their weapons. Theirs may not be the ultimate economic weapon, but where the currency of the world is concerned, it seems to be the universal solvent.

14

Real Money

You have to choose between trusting to the natural stability of gold and the honesty and intelligence of the members of the government. And, with due respect for those gentlemen, I advise you, so long as the capitalist system lasts, to vote for gold.

George Bernard Shaw,
The Intelligent Woman's Guide to Socialism and Capitalism, 1928

At the conclusion of Chapter 1, "What Is Money?" we stated that "for thousands of years gold and silver have been the universally accepted medium of exchange. No Congress nor President, no King nor Parliament can debase their value nor destroy the acceptance of gold and silver as real money."

Today, despite threats, attempted demonetization, legal sanctions, import and export restrictions, and criminal prosecutions by the United States and other governments, gold and silver remain the bedrock repository of monetary value.

Refugees of both world wars who fled their homes and abandoned prized possessions carried concealed on their persons coins and small bars of precious metal which they used in many instances to buy their lives.

When rampant inflation brought financial breakdown in Germany after World War I, the economy was kept from total collapse by trading in bare essentials, which was made possible by the exchange of gold and silver that had been held in safekeeping throughout the war by a few individuals.

Today some people in India, who must do without much that Americans take for granted, risk imprisonment to purchase and own small amounts of the tons of gold which are smuggled into that country each year.

Even before gold ownership became legal for U.S. citizens at the end of 1974, rapidly increasing numbers of American individuals who lived or traveled abroad, scores of large American corporations with overseas offices, and U.S. banks with foreign branches and investments had broken the law to hedge against increasing inflation by owning gold.

In 1511 Spain's King Ferdinand II admonished his explorers of the New World, "Humanely if possible; but at all hazards get gold!"

Today, except perhaps for the hijacking of smuggler caravans crossing into India, there's not much gold to be had by plunder. What little gold remains in the ground is difficult and costly to extract. Its world price is set twice daily in London by a group of five gold firms which constitute the London Gold Market. Their daily price "fixing" is carried out with the formality of a religious ceremony and exerts worldwide influence which has been described as surpassing the influence of the Council of Trent.

The ceremony dates back to September 12, 1919, and includes representatives of Mocatta & Goldsmid, founded in 1684 (and since 1694, silver brokers to the Bank of England); Sharps Pixley & Company; N. M. Rothschild & Sons; Johnson Matthey & Company; and Samuel Montagu & Company, which the London Gold Market's official brochure describes as, "the most recently formed member, established in 1853."

Each morning five men from the Market's five members meet in the offices of Jeffrey Alan, the manager of Rothschild's bullion and foreign exchange department and the first of two daily price "fixings" begins when Alan suggests an opening price, "Gentlemen, we will start at $185.64"—or whatever may be appropriate that morning.

The day's opening price is based on the previous day's closing, plus any new situation developing overnight. Each dealer will have been in contact with his major customers and will have a good feel for the market for the day.

If no one present offers to sell at the opening price it's moved upwards, initially at ten cents an ounce and then by units of five cents until one of the men present offers gold. If there are no buyers at the opening price, it moves down until one of the men in the room offers to buy.

Once trading starts, the price moves marginally until there is enough gold offered to meet the demand. That price becomes the day's opening figure worldwide.

In recent years the volume of United States gold sales have grown to the extent that it now justifies its own "fixing," so the members of the London Gold Market meet a second time during the day, at 3:00 P.M. London time, to fix an updated price for the opening gold trading in the United States.

The daily price of silver is also set in London each

day in a similar, if less ritualized manner, as traders on the London Metal Exchange answer the call to bid, "Silver, gentlemen, silver."

All of this the United States Government chooses to officially ignore. Yet, despite its insistence that gold is just another commodity, the United States has, since August 15, 1971, refused to honor the claims of foreign governments who had been promised that U.S. dollars in their possession could be exchanged for gold. The United States Treasury, it seems, finally decided to hang onto most of its gold for a rainy day.

A few years earlier, Johnson administration Federal Reserve Board Chairman William McChesney Martin had pledged that "the United States will pay out its last bar of the barbarous relic, gold, to honor foreign claims."

The value of gold is something Soviet leaders are in complete agreement about. In 1972 Foreign Trade Minister Sergei Shevchenko stated that "world trade must rest on a more solid foundation than currency and that solid foundation can only be one thing: gold. Gold should be the basis for everything." It's safe to assume that Shevchenko was speaking for his government; he's alive and well and living in Moscow.

Gold has been coveted by man since before the concept of money crossed anyone's mind. Ancient Egyptian reliefs dating from 3000 B.C. depict gold mining. By 200 B.C. gold had become the standard of exchange between Babylonians. Their basic monetary unit, the shekel, was a small ingot with a fixed weight—the equivalent of 8.34 grams—of fine gold.

In 700 B.C. the small industrialized empire of Lydia established the first mint and put its seal on uniform pieces of metal that were 75 per cent gold, 25 per cent alloy. (To the Lydians also goes credit for inventing the game of dice and establishing the first commercial inns —a nice combination for traveling men.)

In 542 B.C. Lydian King Croesus ordered his mint to strike the first coins of pure gold. Since then, gold coins have been minted by nearly every government which has existed during the last twenty-five centuries. For almost as long, since the reign of Alexander the Great of Macedon (336–323 B.C.), silver coins have shared monetary supremacy with gold. But even for years before the first coins, objects of gold and silver were exchanged for goods between traders and were prized possessions to be taken into the next world.

Taking no chances of arriving in his next life as a pauper, Egypt's King Tutankhamen (c. 1358 B.C.) went to his sepulcher in a solid gold coffin weighing 2,400 pounds.

But why gold? Why silver? Because thousands of years of history have proven that gold and silver are the best hedges against inflation and economic instability that exist.

Early kings and emperors, just as susceptible to inflationary temptation as today's politicians, tried to debase coinage to create additional money. Sometimes they succeeded, but, with coins of gold and silver, changes in weight size and fineness were relatively easy to determine and scores of rulers lost their heads or were exiled for attempting to fiddle with the value of the people's money.

In recent years, now that paper currency has replaced real money, gold and silver have served as financial shelter against massive inflation and repeated currency devaluations.

In the 1960s Indonesia's President Achmed Sukarno

consigned his economy to runaway inflation with a public works program paid for with printing-press money. He increased his country's money supply 390,000 per cent and decreased its value to less than 1 per cent of its former worth. During that time the price of silver in Indonesia increased 6,500 times, protecting those who owned it from financial ruin.

During the early 1970s, when Chile's annual inflation rate soared to 300 per cent, the price of silver in Chile increased 1,500 times, preserving the assets of individuals who held silver.

In China, during the 1940s, while rampant inflation of Chiang Kai-Shek's printing-press economy nearly buried China beneath a mountain of paper, the price of silver in China grew 6 million times, making the difference between life and starvation for millions. Two subsequent currency reforms replaced old money with new and each time inflation returned like a vampire to drain away the economic lifeblood of the people. In each instance precious metals meant survival for those who'd had the foresight to acquire them. In May of 1949, when the Communists took over mainland China, rice cost nearly 500 times what it had cost two months before.

Soon after the Russian revolution of November 1917, the Bolsheviks turned to printing-press currency in an effort to solve economic problems. Before long, inflation added its cold grip to the icy clasp of winter and starving people began burning their worthless "*sovznaki*" ruble notes to keep warm during their last days of life. In 1921 Lenin overrode the objections of his comrades and introduced new currency with a fixed value of ten pre-Revolutionary rubles, exchangable for 119.4826 grains of fine gold.

As we mentioned earlier, precious metals kept the economy of Germany alive following World War I. During those days, the price of silver in Germany increased 90 *billion* times. A pound of butter in 1923 cost 6 billion marks—or one small silver coin.

Immediately after World War II, the economy of Communist Hungary was in about the same shape. Bank notes with denominations of one hundred sextillion pengös were in circulation when the government voided all outstanding currency and instituted new currency tied to gold.

One of the first major economic acts of General Charles de Gaulle, when he assumed the presidency of France in 1959, was to revalue the franc 100 to 1—1 new franc for every 100 of the old. He reduced budget deficits and began acquiring gold for the national treasury. By 1967 he was able to restore international convertability, allow unrestricted ownership of gold, and resume gold trading on the Paris bourse.

The Swiss, whose currency is the strongest in the world, have always kept their banknotes tied to gold.

During America's own worsening inflation, silver has continued to prove its value as a protector from inflation. Between August 1973 and February 1974 the price of silver increased 300 per cent. Since 1940 the price of silver in the United States has climbed 600 per cent.

Though Americans were not allowed to own gold, except rare coins and jewelry, between 1933 and the last day of 1974, the value of the metal soared during the years of galloping inflation.

Since 1968, when the worldwide price of gold was decontrolled with the establishment of the "two-tier" international monetary system (one value for gold exchanged between nations, another "floating" value for the free market), the price of gold has outstripped the U.S. rate of inflation.

From $35.00 an ounce in March 1968, the price of gold climbed to $176.00 an ounce by January 1, 1974, when Americans were permitted to legally own it. By October 1975 the price had slipped to $143.30 per ounce. On December 22, 1975 an ounce of gold was selling on international markets for $139.30.

During the fall of 1975 the International Monetary Fund announced that it was considering the sale of some of its own gold to provide loans to developing countries. Although the sale of IMF gold might be expected to maintain, or possibly even lower, short-term gold prices, growing industrial demand and continuing inflation make the metal a valid long-term investment.

For years gold-poor Great Britain and the United States pressured the United Nations forty-four-member International Monetary Fund (IMF), without success, to "demonetize" gold for international trade.

In 1970 the IMF created special drawing rights (SDRs) which were to serve as international legal tender in settling debts between nations. Though not exchangeable for gold, SDRs were pegged to gold, each SDR having a fictitious gold "value" supposedly equal to 0.888671 grams of fine gold.

But already "paper gold" SDRs are in trouble. In 1970 $3.4 billion in SDRs were issued and divided between the original forty-four IMF members. A few months afterward, $2.6 billion more were issued, soon to be followed by another $3.6 billion in 1972.

Although it can be said that, since the IMF has gold reserves, there is some gold backing for SDRs, the new "paper gold" is composed mostly of a "breadbasket" of sixteen currencies, with purely fiat U.S. dollars comprising about one third.

Increasing numbers of IMF nations are becoming disenchanted with SDRs and are hoarding what gold they have. They are even refusing to sell small quantities of gold to other nations who need it to make the required gold deposits with the IMF in order to join the organization.

Operated much like a huge international credit union which makes loans to member nations, the IMF requires that any country wishing to join make a qualifying deposit before being awarded its "credit line" of SDRs, which it can use like money in international trade.

In 1971, when Syria applied for membership in the IMF, she had to go into the free market to buy gold to make her qualifying deposit because no other nation —including the United States—would sell it to her.

In 1972 France and Japan refused to participate in an IMF effort to raise a mere $7 million in gold to provide for the qualifying gold deposits of Bahrein, Qatar, and the United Arab Emirates.

More recently Bangladesh was unable to buy $2 billion in gold for her IMF membership deposit until finally Canada agreed to sell her that amount in exchange for sterling.

Of all European nations, Britain is the only one to hold less gold today than twenty years ago, down from $2.3 billion in 1953 to slightly less than $1 billion at the close of 1974. United States gold reserves have fallen even more drastically; from $24.4 billion in 1953 to about $10 billion in 1974.

Not only has the amount of U.S. gold reserves dwindled, but foreign claims against it have mounted.

In 1948 there were about $7 billion in foreign claims against U.S. gold reserves. By 1957 our reserves had been reduced to $22.6 billion and foreign claims had grown to $12.6 billion. Four years later, in 1961, foreign claim exceeded the amount of U.S. gold reserves. In 1965 our reserves stood at only $15 billion in the face of foreign claims of almost twice that amount, $27 billion.

In two moves during 1965 and 1968, the Johnson administration and Congress eliminated the requirement for 25 per cent gold backing for Federal Reserve deposits and for the 25 per cent gold backing for Federal Reserve notes. As of 1968 U.S. currency became merely fiat "money," banknotes without backing.

A knowledge of the background we've been citing is important because it's critical to understand the following:

Having no backing at all, U.S. currency will continue to decline in relation to gold and silver.

Having no backing at all, U.S. currency will continue to decline in relationship to currencies which are tied to gold. Manufactured goods and raw materials from strong-currency countries will increase in terms of dollars.

As the value of the dollar declines, foreign nations will buy up more and more American goods, bidding up domestic prices and eventually creating shortages in the United States.

Since there is no tie between gold and the value of the dollar, U.S. politicians will continue the inflationary policies of the past.

The fiscal sins of past deficit spending, the massive fiscal 1967 federal deficit, and future deficits built into the economy all but assure that over the long and even medium term the dollar will decline against the value of gold and silver. Nothing short of a 1930s type depression can turn the tide.

The government will initiate additional currency devaluations (at least two during 1975–76); it will impose new foreign exchange restrictions; it will be forced to continue deficit spending; and it may even resort to price controls and rationing.

But laws, restrictions, and regulations cannot create resources nor provide backing for worthless currency.

Growing long-term demand and limited supplies are combining to increase steadily the price of both gold and silver.

The "easy" gold of the 1800s has been mined. And new gold is now being obtained from deep in the ground at great expense. Two of South Africa's newest gold mining companies, Consolidated Gold Fields and the Anglo-American Corporation, expect to tunnel nearly two miles beneath the surface to reach gold-carrying veins of ore.

The world supply of gold is not only limited, but also not particularly large. Total world production of gold up to 1974 is estimated to be less than 100,000 tons. On a good day United States Steel produces 100,000 tons of steel in one hour. Mining analyst A. D. Mutch, of Bell Gouinlock & Company, of Toronto, Canada, points out that both the United States and Australia reached their gold production peak before World War I, Canada during World War II. The U.S.S.R. is probably nearing its peak production years, and South Africa's gold output can be expected to decline by 1990.

(A cubic foot of gold, by the way, weighs half a ton and, at about $175 an ounce, is worth $1,575,000. The world's biggest gold hoard isn't in Fort Knox or its Russian equivalent. It's in the sub-sub-sub-sub-subbasement of the New York branch of (you guessed it) the Federal Reserve Bank, in the heart of the city's financial district. Give them forty-eight hours' notice, and you can see it.)

At last count, the gold bullion in the basement of the New York Federal Reserve Bank totaled twice the amount of all U.S. gold reserves, most of which is in Fort Knox. Very little of the gold in New York is American; most is owned by nearly a hundred nations which keep part of their gold reserves in the United States. Some was shipped to the United States for safekeeping during World War II, but much of it was obtained by foreign governments since the 1950s as a result of continuing U.S. balance of payments deficits. With the exception of France, most foreign governments would just as soon leave their gold in the United States as move it home.

If you decide to visit the Fed's New York gold vaults, you won't be told which of the 120 gray lockers contains whose gold. The Fed maintains strict confidentiality by keeping its records in Swiss numbered accounts. Not even the men who handle the gold know who it belongs to.

On August 14, 1974, when President Ford signed the bill ending America's forty-one-year prohibition against gold-coin ownership by U.S. citizens, which went into effect January 1, 1975, bankers' response was mixed. The nation's chief banker, Treasury Secretary William Simon, expressed the fear that U.S. citizens' right to own gold coin or bullion might result in "disintermediation," governmentese for "increase the flow of money from savings institutions."

On the same day another Treasury Department official, Michael O'Connell, stated that "our basic philosophy is that gold should be treated just like any other commodity" and thus not under the jurisdiction of the Treasury.

Commercial bankers and savings and loan officials quickly issued statements and news releases warning the public against buying gold because bankers would rather have the public's money in deposits (which bankers can lend at a profit) than in gold.

But as one Treasury official pointed out, "all they're worried about is losing the interest they've been charging for lending other people's money. If you withdraw money from your account to purchase gold, obviously they can't lend it to someone and charge them 10 or 12 per cent for it."

In keeping with its policy of discouraging private ownership of gold—which would be disadvantageous for private bankers—the United States Government offered two million ounces of Treasury gold on the open market the very day that Americans were allowed to purchase the yellow metal.

Concurrently, the Federal Reserve Board, the Office of The Comptroller of Currency, and the Federal Deposit Insurance Corporation all sought to discourage banks from selling gold to the public. At the same time, the Securities and Exchange Commission warned the public that investing in gold was a "risky" venture because of unscrupulous dealers who might take advantage of unsophisticated buyers. Considering the SEC's own docket of stock fraud investigations and the millions of individuals' dollars lost in the current recession, the SEC hardly seems to be in a position to warn investors away from gold.

In answer to bankers' and bureaucrats' criticism of gold and silver investments, we need only ask, "What better alternative do you have to offer?" No amount of talk can stem the dollar's long-term depreciation against the "real money" value of gold and silver.

Henry Kaufman, chief economist of the New York investment banking firm of Salomon Brothers, lobbied strong and hard with Senate Economic Growth Sub-Committee Chairman Senator Lloyd M. Bentsen of Texas to forestall the public's right to own gold.

According to Salomon Brothers, "if gold is purchased from U. S. Treasury sales, the proceeds will increase Treasury balances and reduce federal expenditures net, which is a poor way of reducing the budget deficit.

"If gold comes from foreign sources, that will damage the U.S. balance of payments. The efficiency of American mass-merchandising and marketing techniques could make gold sales to U.S. citizens proportionately much higher than to those of other nations which already have legalization. . . .

"That," said Salomon Brothers' Kaufman, "could add to current disintermediation problems by increasing withdrawals from time deposits as investors move into gold . . . Why run the risk now of additional pressures on our financial institutions which may intensify fears about their validity?"

As Dallas, Texas, commodity consultant Eugene Jackson points out, "In other words, if Americans are allowed to choose what they want to do with their money, they might buy some gold and not buy some new debt issues Salomon Brothers wants to peddle. After all, we can't allow common, ordinary American citizens to enjoy that much freedom of choice in the spending of their money . . . or can we?"

By mid-1975, major United States banks, including the Bank of America; Wells Fargo Bank; Continental Illinois National Bank & Trust Company, Chicago; Manufacturers National Bank, Detroit; the American

Bank & Trust Company, New York; the Republic National Bank of New York; and the National Bank of Commerce, Dallas, were selling gold bullion and wafers.

Many small banks such as the Wyoming National Bank, Casper, Wyoming; Kanawha Valley Bank, Charleston, West Virginia; Fourth National Bank & Trust Company, Wichita, Kansas; and the First National Bank, Jackson, Mississippi, also offer "over-the-counter" gold to investors.

Gold can also be purchased through many New York Stock Exchange members such as Bache & Company; Paine, Webber, Jackson & Curtis, Inc.; Reynolds Securities; and others. Wall Street's largest broker—Merrill Lynch, Pierce, Fenner & Smith, Inc.—was quick to take out large newspaper ads headed "Gold: What Every First-Time Investor Should Know."

For years before gold bullion became available as an investment for U.S. citizens, Americans had been investing in silver.

According to Standard & Poor's *Trade and Securities Statistics,* silver prices have shown an almost uninterrupted rise for the past twenty years:

YEAR	PRICE PER TROY OUNCE
1955	$ .89
1956	.91
1957	.91
1958	.89
1959	.91
1960	.91
1961	.92
1962	1.08
1963	1.28
1964	1.29
1965	1.29

YEAR	PRICE PER TROY OUNCE
1966	1.29
1967	1.55
1968	2.14*
1969	1.79
1970	1.77
1971	1.55
1972	1.68
1973	2.54
1974	4.71
1975	4.10†

Increasing silver prices are being generated by three factors which will continue to provide a growing market.

1. *Increasing industrial consumption.* Utilization of silver for manufacturing, medical, electronic, and research uses is expanding almost every year:

YEAR	INDUSTRIAL CONSUMPTION (MILLIONS OF TROY OUNCES)
1962	110
1963	110
1964	123
1965	137
1966	150
1967	145
1968	145
1969	142
1970	128
1971	129
1972	151
1973	190
1974	170

* Year of worldwide gold-buying crisis.
†Temporary drop due to world-wide recession.

2. *Limited Supply.* The amount of silver in the earth is finite, and there is little chance of locating a major new discovery. According to officials of the Sunshine mine, in Idaho, America's largest silver mine, "the chances of finding a major new silver deposit in the U.S. are about ten thousand to one." Today 70 per cent of U.S.-produced silver is obtained as a by-product of refining lead, zinc, and copper ore, and the supply is falling short of demand:

YEAR	ANNUAL SHORTFALL MILLIONS OF TROY OUNCES
1962	—50
1963	—46
1964	—87
1965	—124
1966	—126
1967	—135
1968	—120
1969	—110
1970	—84
1971	—106
1972	—147
1973	—214
1974	—211

3. *Inflation.* The declining purchasing power of United States currency against silver causes the dollar price of silver to increase. Ten thousand dollars invested in silver bullion in 1973 returned $15,025 during 1974.

The declining value and lack of backing for U.S. currency have already made it an unacceptable medium of exchange on some international markets. Most member nations of the Organization of Petroleum Exporting Countries (OPEC), announced during the fall of 1974 that they would no longer accept U.S. currency, nor

British pounds, for that matter, in exchange for oil. They will, however, accept silver—and gold.

Texas oilman Bunker Hunt, son of recently deceased oilman H. L. Hunt, has been investing heavily in silver bullion since 1973. According to reports (Mr. Hunt gives out little data on his silver purchases), the millionaire owned more than 50 million ounces during 1974 and has made paper profits of more than $200 million. Charles R. Stahl, publisher of *Green's Commodity Market Comment,* describes Hunt's silver investment "the biggest commodity coup ever made."

The rumor, reported in the March 25, 1974, issue of *Barron's,* the financial magazine, that the Hunt family was making arrangements with the Arabs to exchange silver for crude oil at the rate of two ounces of silver for one barrel of oil has never been proved nor disproved.

When interviewed by *Barron's* during April 1974, Hunt declined to talk about possible oil deals, but did give his evaluation of the future of paper assets: "Just about anything you can buy, rather than paper, is better. You're bound to come out ahead in the long pull. If you don't like gold, use silver, or diamonds, or copper, or anything. Any damn fool can run a printing press. . . . It's the 'screwballs' and the goldbugs who have been right."

There are a number of alternatives to investing in gold and silver bullion: coins, commodity futures, mining company stock, and, most recently, gold certificates.

Gold and silver coins have appreciated tremendously over the years and will continue to do so, and there's no harm in having several hundred dollars in silver U.S. coins hidden away for use as pocketmoney in the event of predicted total financial collapse which will bring about the complete nonacceptance of paper money.

But, as an investment medium during runaway inflation and threatened economic collapse, coins have severe limitations. No silver coin that we know of is of acceptable monetary purity. Pre-1964 United States silver coins, for example, were only .900 fine, far less than the .999 purity required for monetary bullion.

Coins which have been in circulation a long time often lose 10 per cent of their weight due to wear. Another 5 per cent is lost during smelting required to meet standards for .999 purity.

Finally, there is almost always a premium on silver coins over and above their intrinsic value. The premium is the amount of a coin's value to coin collectors over and above the value of its silver content. The premium may be worth something to collectors, but it means nothing when you have to exchange it for bread or sell it to a smelter or industrial silver user during a monetary crisis.

Gold coins are usually quite pure, but there is also a premium on them which collectors must pay, over and above the gold value of the coin.

Here are a few gold coins, their gold weights, and their coin-collectors' premiums over and above their gold value:

COUNTRY	COIN	TROY OZ. GOLD	PER CENT PREMIUM
United States	$20 Liberty "Double Eagle"	.96746	70
Great Britain	Sovereign (£1)	.23540	30
France	20-franc	.18666	40
Italy	20-lira	.18666	120
Mexico	50-peso	1.20563	25

Increasing numbers of gold coins are being restruck by the nations that originally minted them. Dates on the new coins are not the current ones but those of the original minting, so that these "counterfeit" gold coins are indistinguishable from genuine collector's items. Mexico is know to be restriking 50-peso gold pieces. Austria, Great Britain, Hungary, France, Liechtenstein, India, Spain, Switzerland, and Turkey are all restriking supposedly "old" gold coins.

Donald C. Hoppe, author of *How to Invest in Gold Coins* (Arlington House, 1973), warns potential investors that "the production of coin restrikes by some governments is one of the less appealing facts of life with which coin investors must learn to live. There are several motives for issuing restrikes. One is simply to take advantage of numismatic demand for certain rare coins. Another obvious reason is to satisfy the demand for gold coin merely as bullion.

"Some government restrikes are marked to identify them in some way, but others are not. . . . However, at the risk of sounding cynical . . . I must observe that those very minute identification marks can be most easily removed by a skilled jeweler or engraver."

Silver coins, like their gold sisters, often command a premium over and above their intrinsic value. The standard trading unit is a fifty-five-pound bag of silver dimes, quarters, and halves with a face value of $1,000. The premium on even this "junk silver," as dealers call bags containing no rare or collectors' value coins, is about 10 per cent. To this figure a coin dealer will add his normal profit plus a 2 per cent commission based on a price somewhat above the intrinsic value of the coins, plus the dealer's shipping and packing expenses, usually about $40.00 per bag.

Mining stocks seem to offer good investment possibilities, but the fallacy in owning stocks is that all you really own is a stake in the potential profits of the company. No profits, no dividends, and no stock appreciation.

Although silver continued to appreciate during the past few years, an investment in the common stock of the Sunshine Mining Company would have yielded a loss. During 1973 the Idaho mine suffered a major fire which put it out of operation for several months. In 1974 the same mine underwent a prolonged strike over safety conditions and was again shut down for some time.

Flooding of one of the shafts of the East Driefontein Gold Mining Company in South Africa during 1972 shut down the mine for nearly four years. It is a mistake to own stock; there is a more direct way to own the means of profit from gold and silver.

To cite another example, when Edward Schaffer, publisher of the respected *Dow Theory Trader,* advised subscribers during 1974 that he was removing gold and silver stocks from the theoretical portfolios he maintained, his words amounted to a suggestion to sell.

A firestorm of orders to sell gold and silver issues hit Wall Street the next trading day and before the closing bell some stocks lost 50 per cent of their value. The stock of ASA, Limited, a South African investment firm specializing in gold mining shares, fell from 89.62 to 52.12. The shares of America's largest gold and silver mines suffered similar defeats.

Of all possible modes of precious-metals investment, the buying and selling of futures on the commodities markets are perhaps the most dangerous.

Silver is traded at the New York Commodities Exchange in minimum contracts of 10,000 troy ounces each; and at the Chicago Board of Trade in minimum contracts of 5,000 troy ounces each.

Gold is traded at the New York Commodities Exchange in minimum 100-ounce contracts and at the Chicago Board of Trade in minimum contracts of 50 ounces.

Margin requirements at both exchanges are between 6 and 10 per cent.

Contracts to buy and sell silver and gold on future dates at fixed prices are purchased through a commodity broker or the commodity specialist at large stock brokerage houses. Since the commodity market moves much more quickly than the stock market, speculators must be prepared to cover their margins almost instantly in the case of a price drop or risk being sold out.

Successful commodities trading requires large amounts of *risk* capital, excellent timing, and the ability to foresee and properly evaluate a broad spectrum of factors which could affect the market. It is a full-time job for professionals. Harry Browne, well-known financial consultant and author of the best-selling book, *You Can Profit from a Monetary Crisis* (Macmillan, 1974), cautions readers that "for most people the task [of commodities trading] is too difficult."

C. M. Allen, the New York management consultant who wrote *How to "Wheel & Deal" in Gold & Silver* (1973) warns that "you must watch the commodity game minute by minute." Commodity markets swing enormously up and down in quick periods of time, so if you don't have the time to keep on top of your investment you must find someone whom you trust implicitly to do so for you. If the stock market is like making a bet at the track, the commodity market is like making a bet and then having to ride your horse.

Gold certificates are now being sold in the United States by a number of banks. The certificates simply promise to deliver to the owner on demand a predetermined amount of gold. Similar certificates have been sold for years to Canadians (and to Americans) by the Bank of Nova Scotia in Canada. They are a form of investment, since they are for a predetermined *amount* of gold rather than for a fixed dollar *value.*

The certificates must be redeemed by the seller, will not be replaced if lost, and can easily be destroyed. At any time the government could require issuing banks to register and report all redemptions or transfers, could declare a "holiday" on redemptions, and could impose a tax. Transfer to heirs is also complicated, since gold certificates, like stock certificates, must be endorsed by the owner whenever they change hands.

The ownership of bullion kept in a safe place avoids many of these dangers and restrictions. The "real money" of gold and silver bullion can easily be purchased from banks and other reliable institutions. Price offerings are of nearly exact monetary quality, .999 fine, and gold and silver bullion is nearly indestructible and can be transferred to heirs or others without paperwork or signed endorsement.

"Gold and silver," someone once said, "are the ultimate money because they are the only assets that aren't someone else's liability. They don't represent someone else's promise to pay and they don't depend upon the survival of any particular power or group of powers."

In short, gold and silver are *real money.*

15

Who's in Charge Here?

I don't know what my profession is coming to. The ancient kings had necromancers, prophets and soothsayers. Nowadays we have economists performing the same function for Presidents. The efficacy of one group is perhaps no greater than that of the other.

Arthur Burns, Chairman,
Federal Reserve Board

This is the place, in many books, where the author outlines his solutions for the weighty problems he had been discussing for two or three hundred pages. Unfortunately I can't do that because I don't believe there is any cure for the nation's fiscal ills which our weakened economic system can withstand.

Our debilitated fiscal condition is similar to that of a critically ill patient whose sickness has been allowed to progress so far that any potential cure is likely to prove fatal.

There is so little agreement among our national policy makers that practically no effective economic initiative can be taken. Up until December 1975, despite the universally acknowledged pressing need, there was, after nearly two years of political bickering, no consensus between the President and Congress on any plan for facing the nation's energy crisis.

When high-level energy statements have been made, we're soon given reason to doubt them:

> "If anybody in Congress wants to impose an excise tax that will raise the price of gasoline, it will have to be over my dead body."
>
> President Ford, October 1974.

> "I have informed the Congress of my intention to levy a graduated tax on oil as a means of reducing consumption of petroleum products."
>
> President Ford, February 1975.

Whatever political compromise is finally agreed upon, it can do little to compensate for the long-range inflationary effect of the increased cost of petroleum and the shortages and higher prices of many items.

In other economic areas—foreign wheat sales (which raise the price of nearly all foods since farmers shift from growing green vegetables to growing wheat and from growing cattle feed to growing wheat), taxation, welfare, and the money supply (controlled by the Federal Reserve Board)—continuing disagreement and political bickering hamper the implementation of measures which just might help our economy pull through.

The analogy is an old one, but one can easily imagine the good ship of our national economy floundering in a deepening sea of deficit, the crew running about the decks in conflict and panic while no one mans the wheel.

During 1975 Senator Hubert Humphrey, chairman of the Joint Economic Committee, proposed a $30-billion tax cut as a means of increasing the GNP and reducing unemployment.

As soon as the Humphrey proposal became known, Alan Greenspan, chairman of the Council of Economic Advisers, pointed out that the tax cut would raise the GNP only 1.5 to 2 points and would reduce unemployment only 0.5 to 0.8 percentage points below forecast figures. The price of so small a gain, however, would be an additional $20 billion tacked on to the $70-billion estimated national debt for fiscal 1976.

While both houses of Congress were passing a major tax cut, Federal Reserve Board Chairman Arthur Burns counseled President Ford to veto the $23-billion tax reduction legislation, arguing that it would sow the seeds of a new inflationary binge.

While Dr. Burns cautioned the President against following the legislative lead of Congress, Representative Henry Reuss, chairman of the powerful House Committee on Banking, voiced the opinion of many influential congressional leaders when he stated: "It has been the stop and go policy of the Federal Reserve Board which has been a major cause of inflation combined with excessive unemployment."

In the Senate, Joint Economic Committee Chairman Humphrey declared: "The tight money and high interest rates of the Federal Reserve Board have not halted inflation. They have added to it. They have choked off economic growth, brought home-building to a virtual standstill, increased bankruptcies among businessmen and farmers, and have created havoc in our capital markets."

During 1975, Congress fired a warning shot across the bow of the Federal Reserve by declaring in a rare joint resolution:

"The Congress of the United States hereby directs its agents, the Board of Governors of the Federal Reserve and the Open Market Committee to:

(1) Take appropriate action . . . to increase the money supply at a rate substantially higher than recent experience . . .

(2) Maintain long-term growth of the money supply commensurate with the economy's long-run potential to increase production . . .

The joint resolution also called upon the Federal Reserve Board to consult with Congress at semiannual hearings before the committees on banking about its money-supply growth targets.

Chairman Burns seems to have little patience with congressional meddling in national fiscal or monetary affairs. "The Congress," he states, "has not found it easy to legislate fiscal policy. If the Congress now seeks to legislate monetary policy as well, it would enter a vastly more intricate, highly sensitive, and rapidly changing field—with consequences that could prove very damaging to our nation's economy." Clearly, Chairman Burns feels that economics is too important to be left to the politicians.

However, there is wide disagreement even among leading economists called before the Senate Banking Committee to advise on money supply goals. Herbert Stein, chairman of the Council of Economic Advisers under President Nixon, told the Senate Banking Committee that the nation's money supply should be allowed to grow at the rate of 9 per cent per year through 1978.

Other respected economists such as Dr. Carl Christ of Johns Hopkins University and Beryl Sprinkle, executive vice president of the Harris Trust and Savings Bank of Chicago, advocated a money-supply growth rate of only 3 or 4 per cent in their testimony before the same committee.

As a senior member of President Ford's own party, former Republican presidential nominee Senator Barry Goldwater would like to support the President's 1976 budget, but finds he can't. "I see nothing but complete disaster," says Goldwater, "in President Ford's 1976 budget because I don't believe the nation's economy can stand that kind of attack on its solvency."

Referring to the 1976 budget's estimated $70-billion deficit, Goldwater said, "I do not know any way in the world that an individual can continue to spend money he does not have, or a government can continue to spend money that it does not have, without eventually going bankrupt.

"The total debt of this country, including Federal debt, State debt, local debt, and our own personal debts, is more money than we now have. So it gets to be rather simple arithmetic; the country, if it continues the spending that it is engaged in, is going to have to print more money . . ."

Declaring that the fate of the dollar is too important to be left in the hands of economists and "intellectual dreamers," Goldwater argues for a return to the gold standard. "I know the gold standard is far from perfect," he says, "but it shines brightly in comparison with what we have today."

While there might be reasoned disagreement with nearly every economic policy presented by Congress, the Federal Reserve Board, and the President, continuing disagreement and inaction deflates the long-term value of your dollar just as surely as no policy at all.

There is little hope that the United States will return to the gold standard in the foreseeable future, so while we can not conclude this book with a list of cures for the fiscal disease which infects our national economy, we can suggest that some measure of personal financial safety can be found in turning away from easily printed paper currency toward the "real money" of gold and silver.

GLOSSARY

Balance of payments The sum total of the nation's financial relationships with the rest of the world, measuring what foreigners spend here against what Americans spend abroad. The balance is said to be in surplus if foreigners spend more here, in deficit if Americans spend more abroad.

Balance of trade The record of the difference between what foreigners spend for American goods and what Americans spend for imported foreign goods. If exports exceed imports, the balance is in surplus; if imports exceed exports, it is in deficit. The balance of trade is the major component of the balance of payments.

Budget deficit A situation in which the government spends more than it takes in through taxes and other revenue. Governments finance deficits by borrowing from the public. The interest on the public debt becomes part of government spending in future years.

Budget surplus The result when a government collects more than it spends in a year. It can use the excess to pay off some of the federal debt or increase its cash reserves.

Bullion Monetary gold or silver in an uncoined state, usually consisting of bars or ingots, .999 fine.

Capital investment Spending for plant and equipment that is used in the future production of other goods. When an oil company builds a refinery, it is investing in capital goods. Capital investment can be done to replace worn-out plant and equipment or can be an addition to society's capacity to produce.

Community rehabilitation loans Loans that are directed to providing housing and employment opportunities for low- and moderate-income persons.

Constant dollars The attempt to remove the impact of price changes from statistics that are reported in dollars.

Consumer price index A statistic that measures the change in price of a selected market basket of goods assumed to be purchased by the average urban worker with a wife and two children. Often called the cost of living index.

Consumption That portion of the nation's output of goods and services that is used up rather than saved. Food is consumed, capital investment is saved.

Counterfeit False coin or banknotes minted or printed with the intent to commit fraud.

Credit allocation Government channeling of loans to specified priority areas such as housing or industrial expansion either by ordering banks to lend the money or by inducing them to make loans by such methods as special tax treatment.

Credit union A co-operative nonprofit organization of individuals with a common bond of occupation, association, or residence. Its purpose is to promote thrift among its members and to provide them with a source of credit at reasonable rates.

Currency Paper money, i.e., receipts for real money, that is gold and silver, that the issuer has in storage.

Debase To reduce the value of a banknote or coin while maintaining its face value. Currency devaluations are a form of debasement; inflation debases currency. Reducing the weight or fineness of gold or silver debases coins.

Deflation A decrease in the amount of money in circulation relative to the amount of gold or silver in storage as backing.

Demand deposits Demand deposits, unlike savings and time deposits, are payable at any time upon the depositor's order. Most typically, a demand deposit is a checking account.

Demonetize To withdraw the status as legal tender from coin or currency.

Depreciation An accounting procedure that permits businessmen to deduct from profits as an expense the amount of plant and equipment used up in producing goods. During periods of raging inflation, businessmen debate whether depreciation deductions should be related to the cost of the equipment when they purchased it or what it will cost them to replace it when it wears out.

Devaluation Saying, in effect, "I will no longer redeem my currency for the amount of gold that I promised I would." Devaluation is usually planned without informing the public and announced only at the moment of its initiation.

Discount rate The interest the Federal Reserve System charges a member bank that borrows from it for a short period of time.

Discretionary income The amount of a person's income that remains after he meets all his basic needs and commitments such as food, clothing, shelter, taxes, and debt payments.

Disintermediation A situation in which depositors take their money out of banks or savings and loan associations to get a higher return from other investments.

Dual banking system The existence of both federal and state laws and agencies for chartering and supervising financial institutions. Such a system now exists for commercial banks, mutual savings and loan associations, and credit unions. However, under the present law, there is no provision for federal chartering of stock savings and loan associations or mutual savings banks.

Exchange controls Government restrictions on the export and/or import of certain currencies.

FHA and VA interest ceilings The Secretary of Housing and Urban Development and the Chief of the Veterans Administration are empowered to set a maximum rate of interest which may be charged on FHA-insured or VA-guaranteed loans, respectively.

Fiat money Currency which serves as a medium of exchange only because of the power of the state to compel its acceptance, which is not backed by silver or gold, and hence is without real value. Currency which is legal tender because a government says it is.

Financial intermediary A deposit institution such as a bank, savings and loan association, savings bank, or credit union. Its function is to accept deposits from individuals, corporations, or organizations and to make loans with those funds or otherwise to invest them. The earnings from these loans are passed on as interest payments to the depositors and profits or reserve additions to the intermediary.

Fiscal policy The changing of taxes and spending by the government to offset ups and downs in production, employment, and prices. The goal of fiscal policy, as well as of monetary policy, is to achieve full employment without inflation.

Fiscal year An accounting period for the federal government which begins on July 1 and ends on June 30. (E.g., fiscal 1976 began July 1, 1975, and ends June 30, 1976.)

Fixed exchange rates Currency exchange rates which do not vary; either by international agreement or because governments buy and sell each other's currency to balance supply and demand.

Floating exchange rates Currency exchange rates which freely fluctuate in the absence of international agreements or when governments do not buy and sell each others' currency in an effort to balance supply and demand.

Full employment State of the economy when the unemployment rate is relatively low (conventionally, about 4 per cent of the labor force) and production is close to capacity.

GNP, or gross national product The dollar value of the goods and services produced by the economy in a given year. The "real" GNP adjusts that dollar value for changes in prices, in order to measure the increase or decrease in the physical volume of goods and services produced between different years. The GNP is the broadest measure of the health of an economy.

Gold certificate A document which serves as a receipt for gold bullion and for which the issuer promises to deliver a fixed amount of gold in exchange for the certificate.

Gold standard A monetary standard based upon gold backing for currency.

Grain A unit of weight. There are 480 grains in a troy ounce, the standard measure for gold and silver. The troy ounce is slightly heavier (42½ grains heavier) than the avoirdupois ounce. See Troy weight.

Housing starts The number of new dwelling units—apartments or houses—being begun by builders.

Inflation An increase in the amount of currency in circulation relative to the amount of gold and silver backing.

Liquidity The ease with which an individual or company may convert assets to money. Cash and checking accounts are "perfectly liquid." Stocks are much less liquid.

Monetary policy The influence which the Federal Reserve Board exercises over the money supply and, in turn, the flow of credit and the level of interest rates in the economy. The basic tools the Federal Reserve uses are the purchase and sale of government securities in the open market, the discount rate, and raising or lowering the amount of deposits banks cannot lend out.

Money Almost anything that is generally accepted as a medium of exchange. Today this includes currency, personal and corporate checks, gold and silver, bank deposits, and short-term Treasury bills.

Money supply The total of currency and checking accounts held by the public, called M1 by economists. A broader concept, called M2, includes savings deposits at banks.

Mutual savings banks Mutual savings banks may be chartered in eighteen states and Puerto Rico; federal charters are not available to mutual savings banks under the present law. Mutual savings banks have more liberal loan and investment powers than savings and loan associations and in six states may accept demand deposits; however, most of their assets are held in real estate loans.

Mutual thrift institutions These are mutual savings banks and mutual savings and loan associations.

National income The total earnings of individuals and companies that come about from the production of goods and services.

Numismatics The study of coins and other forms of gold and silver "real money" by collectors.

"Old-time religion" Term used to describe the view that the way to fight inflation is to tighten credit, reduce government spending, and balance the budget—accepting some degree of recession if necessary.

OPEC Organization of Petroleum Exporting Countries, which is composed of Algeria, Ecuador, Indonesia, Iran, Iraq, Kuwait, Libya, Nigeria, Qatar, Saudi Arabia, Venezuela, and the United Arab Emirates. Gabon is an associate member.

Points Points are a method of increasing the effective rate of interest on a mortgage loan when contract rates are held below current market rates by state usury limits or administrative ceilings on FHA- or VA-backed loans. A point is 1 per cent of the total value of a mortgage loan.

Premium With respect to gold and silver coins, the difference between the selling price of the coin and the market value of the gold or silver it contains.

Prime rate The interest banks charge their best corporate customers for short-term loans.

Productivity Total output divided by total man-hours worked. Increasing productivity is supposed to make society wealthier because it gets more goods for the same amount of work.

Public service employment Government acting as the employer of last resort for individuals who lose their jobs because of a downturn in economic output.

Real income Purchasing power of earnings or income, adjusted for the inflation in consumer prices. Real spendable earnings also exclude tax payments.

Recession A period in which the economy's output of goods and services undergoes a prolonged, deep decline. For convenience, many economists consider a recession a decline in real gross national product which continues on for more than six months.

Reserve requirements The Federal Reserve Board sets for member banks percentage requirements for demand deposits, savings deposits, and time deposits which member banks must hold in cash or noninterest-bearing deposits at the Federal Reserve. The Federal Reserve Board sets the reserve requirements for each class of deposits within statutory ranges set by Congress. In most states nonmember banks are required to hold reserves; however, they are usually able to hold them in either government obligations or deposits in other commercial banks.

Restrike A coin struck from an original or exact duplicate of an original die by the government which minted the original coin. Nearly all gold restrikes currently circulating among collectors bear dates of the original minting and, in the legal and moral sense, are counterfeit coins produced by the nation which minted the originals.

Revaluation The opposite of devaluation, whereby a government requires fewer units of its currency in exchange for a fixed amount of gold.

Savings accounts Savings deposits are interest-bearing deposits not required by contract to be left on deposit for any specified period of time. Normally, funds in savings accounts may be withdrawn at any time; however, the depositor *may* be required to give at least thirty-days' notice before withdrawal.

Spot price The current, wholesale price of a commodity, most often used with respect to gold and silver bullion.

Stabilization policy Any economic adjustments adopted by government in an attempt to keep employment, production, and prices from fluctuating excessively. It can include monetary, fiscal, or incomes policies or any combination of the three.

Stagflation A word coined several years ago to describe a situation in which output is constant or falling (stagnation) but prices are rising (inflation).

Third-party payment services Any mechanism whereby a deposit institution transfers a depositor's funds to a third party upon the negotiable or nonnegotiable order of the depositor. Checking accounts are the most common type of third-party payment services.

Thrift institutions For the purpose of the President's recommendations, the term "thrift institutions" is reserved for savings and loan associations (S & Ls) and mutual savings banks (MSBs).

Troy weight The system of weight measurement for gold and silver bullion:

24 grains	equals	1 pennyweight
20 pennyweights	equals	1 troy ounce (480 grains)
12 troy ounces	equals	1 troy pound (5,760 grains)

Wholesale price index A statistic that tries to measure the over-all change in the prices of a wide variety of materials used by manufacturers or processors in production. It is generally considered a precursor of prices the consumers ultimately will pay.

BIBLIOGRAPHY

Allen, C. M. *How to "Wheel & Deal" in Gold & Silver.* New York: C. M. Allen, 1973.

Back, George. *Inflation: A Study in Economics, Ethics and Politics.* Providence, R.I.: Brown University Press, 1973.

Biven, W. Carl. *Readings in Economics.* New York: Charles E. Merrill, 1970.

Bloom, Murray. *Rogues to Riches: The Trouble with Wall Street.* New York: G. P. Putnam's Sons, 1972.

Browne, Harry. *You Can Profit from a Monetary Crisis.* New York: Macmillan, 1974.

FDIC *Annual Report.* Washington, D.C.: Federal Deposit Insurance Corporation, 1973

Friedman, Milton. *Dollars and Deficits: Living with America's Economic Problems.* New York: Prentice-Hall, 1968.

Green, Timothy. *The World of Gold Today.* New York: Walker, 1974.

Hazlitt, Henry. *What You Should Know About Inflation.* New York: Funk & Wagnalls, 1968.

Hoppe, Donald. *How To Invest in Gold Coins.* New Rochelle, N.Y.: Arlington House, 1973.

Janeway, Eliot. *The Economics of Crisis: War, Politics and the Dollar.* New York: Weybright and Tally, 1973.

———. *What Shall I Do With My Money?* New York: David McKay, 1970.

Kenan, H. S. *The Federal Reserve Bank.* Los Angeles, Calif.: Noontide Press, 1968.

Krefetz, Gerald. *The Dying Dollar.* Chicago: Playboy Press, 1972

Leong, Y. S. *Silver: An Analysis of Factors Affecting Its Price.* Dubuque, Iowa: William C. Brown, 1933.

Meadows, D. H., et al. *The Limits to Growth.* New York: New American Library, 1972.

Okun, Arthur. *Economic Activity.* Washington, D.C.: Brookings Institution, 1973.

Palyi, Melchior. *The Inflation Primer.* Chicago: Henry Regnery, 1973.

Pick, Franz. *Gold: How and Where to Buy and Hold It.* New York: Pick Publishing Company, 1973.

———. *Silver: How and Where to Buy and Hold It.* New York: Pick Publishing Company, 1974

Proxmire, William. *Uncle Sam, the Last of the Big Time Spenders.* New York: Simon and Schuster, 1972.

Regan, Donald. *A View from the Street.* New York: New American Library, 1972.

Segal, Ronald. The Decline and Fall of the American Dollar. New York: Bantam Books, 1974.

Smith, Adam. *Supermoney.* New York: Random House, 1972.

Stekler, Herman. *Economic Forecasting.* New York: Praeger, 1972.

Welfling, Weldon. *Money and Banking.* New York: American Institute of Banking, 1965.

Wernette, John. *Growth and Prosperity Without Inflation.* New York: Macmillan, 1973.

Woytinsky, Emma. *Profile of the U. S. Economy: A Survey of the Growth and Change.* New York: Praeger, 1972.

INDEX